The Mystery Kept Hidden
for Ages and Generations

The Mystery Kept Hidden for Ages and Generations

THE WEEKS IN SCRIPTURE

Stephen Wright

RESOURCE *Publications* • Eugene, Oregon

Dedicated to Jane Ann Wright, the love of my life
11-22-1963 to 3-21-2023

She threw kindness like confetti . . .
at everyone.

Even the mystery which hath been hid from ages and from generations, but now is made manifest to his saints.

—Colossians 1:26

Open thou mine eyes, that I may behold wondrous things out of thy law.

—Psalm 119:18

There is no clear reason why particular psalms were designated to be
recited on different days of the week. The rabbinic view, found in the
Talmud, connects each psalm to a different day on the basis of hints to
each day of Creation found in the psalms, but often these connections
are not clearly indicated in the psalm's actual text. . . . These interpreta-
tions all seem forced and largely unconvincing. . . . While these psalms
are recited today as a remembrance of the Temple service, the reason
why they were originally chosen remains a mystery. . . .

—Rabbi Dr. Raymond Apple, "The Psalms of the Day"

Let us suppose we possess parts of a novel or a symphony. Someone
now brings us a newly discovered piece of manuscript and says, 'This
is the missing part of the work.['] . . . [I]f it were genuine then at
every fresh hearing of the music or every fresh reading of the book,
we should find it settling down, making itself more at home and
eliciting significance from all sorts of details in the whole work which
we had hitherto neglected. Even though the new central chapter or
main theme contained great difficulties in itself, we should still think
it genuine provided that it continually removed difficulties elsewhere.
. . . The credibility will depend on the extent to which the doctrine, if
accepted, can illuminate and integrate that whole mass.

—C. S. Lewis, *Miracles*

Contents

1.

The Concept: Proof vs. Faith

THIS LITTLE WORK WALKS a path that Scripture points to but does not explore, a road acknowledged but not taken. Here we try to walk that pathway, to take that road. The idea originated when I noticed an anomaly in the Scripture, in the writings of Luke, that at first puzzled me, then captured my imagination. Luke repeatedly tells us that no lesser persons than Jesus and Paul provided proof to their listeners that all Scripture points to the Christ, and to his sacrifice (see Luke 24:25–27, 44–46; Acts 9:22; 17:1–3; 18:28; 26:22–23).

"Proof!" Luke tells us, from Scripture, no less. He does not say the gospel is unprovable and must be accepted on faith. Instead, Luke says that Scripture can be used to prove the gospel and that Jesus and Paul each did just that. Not just faith, mind you. Luke says Jesus and Paul *proved* what we take as unprovable, what we say must be accepted on faith because it cannot be proven.

But Luke does not tell us *how* it was proven. We strain to hear what Jesus said, what Paul offered as proof. But Luke stands mute. He does not tell us how the proof must be marshalled, how Scripture removes belief from the category of faith to that of evidentiary proof. And that omission is the anomaly. It is what we desperately want to hear and assess for ourselves, but Luke does not expound.

1

And that silence disappoints—especially today. We live today in a world of skepticism, where so many tend, not to faith, the substance of things hoped for, but insist instead on ironclad proof before they believe most anything. Luke tells us Jesus and Paul offer such proof, but he declines (no doubt intentionally) to recount their offers of proof.

For instance, in the wonderful Easter passage of Cleopas and his friend on the road to Emmaus, Luke tells how Jesus, with his identity veiled, joins Cleopas and his friend as they walk the short distance from Jerusalem to Cleopas's hometown of Emmaus. On this mystical first Easter Sunday, Cleopas and his friend are distraught but intrigued. They have watched Jesus suffer gruesomely and die on the cross. They have seen all their hopes shattered. But they have heard a peculiar rumor that women went to the tomb that Sunday morning and found the stone rolled away and the dark cave empty. They do not know what is transpiring, but they find it odd indeed.

Cleopas and his friend are joined by Jesus, but they do not recognize him. The unrecognized Jesus asks why they appear so downcast, and they pour out their hearts with a bittersweet recitation of how they just knew that Jesus was the Christ, the messiah for whom they had waited, but that, to their utter dismay, they had seen him die cruelly, shattering their dreams. They are aghast that their visitor, Jesus with identity veiled, has not heard of the terrible things that have happened that week in Jerusalem. Then Luke gives us a verse that stirs our hearts and leaves us wanting more information. Jesus says to them, "O fools, and slow of heart to believe all that the prophets have spoken: Ought not Christ to have suffered these things, and to enter into his glory? And beginning at Moses and all the prophets, he expounded unto them in all the scriptures the things concerning himself" (Luke 24:25–27).

In other words, Luke tells us that Jesus walked alongside Cleopas and his friend and explained to them how Old Testament Scripture pointed directly to his sacrifice and crucifixion. As readers, we want to know exactly what Jesus said. We can certainly imagine that he recounted the prophecies of Moses and the

Servant Songs of Isaiah. That much would seem certain to us, but we are struck with the certainty that Jesus had much more to say than to recount Isaiah. We want to hear Luke go on and tell us that in his interviews and research in the preparation of the Gospel of Luke he has talked to Cleopas and/or Cleopas's friend. We want to learn that they outlined for Luke those Scriptures to which Jesus referred. We want to read from the hand of Luke what Jesus said to those two disappointed disciples, to hear from Jesus's own mouth how Scripture should have told them what was to happen that week in Jerusalem.

But Luke is silent. Nowhere in the Gospel does Luke lay out for us what Jesus said to Cleopas and his friend. Certainly, Cleopas and his friend would never forget what Jesus said. And we certainly know, from the introductions to Luke and to Acts, that Luke was a zealous historian, interviewing those who knew Jesus and the leaders of the early church, to provide for us his Gospel and his history of the Jerusalem church and Paul's early missionary journeys (Acts). Given Luke's research and his thoroughness, we can expect, and hope, that Luke will give us the details. But he does not. Not this time.

This is not the only time that Luke tantalizes us. Later in that same final chapter of the Gospel of Luke, Luke portrays the risen Christ appearing before his disciples in the upper room telling them, "This is what I told you while I was still with you: Everything must be fulfilled that is written about me in the law of Moses, the prophets and the Psalms" (Luke 24:44 NIV). Luke summarizes the content of Jesus's address saying, "Then he opened their minds so they could understand the Scriptures" (Luke 24:45 NIV). Again, Luke teases us, telling us that Jesus explained the Scriptures and showed how they pointed to his sacrifice and his death. But Luke does not share the details.

Elsewhere, in Acts, Luke tells us that Paul, the great apostle to the gentiles, likewise offered his Jewish audiences definitive and logical proof that Old Testament Scripture anticipated God's plan of salvation, that Christ would suffer and die, not come as conquering hero. For instance, in Acts 9, Luke recounts the conversion of Paul and tells us that the recently converted Paul, converted so recently that he still was known by his Jewish name Saul, could prove by Scripture that Jesus is the Christ. Says Luke: "Yet Saul grew more and more powerful and baffled the Jews living in Damascus by *proving* that Jesus is the Messiah" (Acts 9:22 NIV, emphasis added). And again, years later, when Paul was deep into his committed missionary role, Luke describes Paul's work in Thessalonica. Luke tells us that Thessalonica, a city in Greece, had a Jewish synagogue, and, "as was his custom, Paul went into the synagogue, and on three Sabbath days he reasoned with them from the Scriptures, *explaining and proving* that the Messiah had to suffer and rise from the dead" (Acts 17:2–3 NIV, emphasis added). And, much later in Paul's life, as he endured a Roman prison, Paul met with the Jewish leaders of the great city Rome. Luke tells us that those Jews "arranged to meet Paul on a certain day . . . [in] the place where he was staying. He witnessed to them from morning till evening, explaining about the kingdom of God, and from the Law of Moses and from the Prophets he tried to persuade them about Jesus" (Acts 28:23 NIV). Luke even tells us that still other powerful preachers had the ability to take Old Testament Scripture and logically analyze it to show that ancient Scripture forewarned us of God's plan of salvation, how the Christ was to come, not as conquering hero, but as a suffering servant and sacrificial Lamb. Luke tells us that Apollos, a great and persuasive speaker, on arriving in the Greek city of Achaia, "vigorously refuted his Jewish opponents in public debate, *proving* from the Scriptures that Jesus was the Messiah" (Acts 18:27–28 NIV, emphasis added).

In each of these passages Luke tells us that the ancient Christian evangelists, even Christ himself, laid out a logical exposition of Old Testament Scripture that proved Jesus to be the Christ and that foretold his death on the cross. Nowhere, however, does Luke provide the step-by-step analysis by which we can follow that proof. On first thought, we conclude that we are the lesser for the absence of this explanation, an explanation which would make it so much easier, we think, to believe in the Christ and to evangelize the world.

On second thought, however, perhaps it is to our advantage. Certainly, if we accept the premise that the Scripture is God breathed, inspired for our edification, we assume that there is a purpose behind Luke's omission. Certainly, we can all offer our own theories as to why Luke omitted to provide us these tantalizing details, but my conclusion is this: the Holy Spirit did not want us to have Luke's mathematical proof text because the Holy Spirit wants us to construct our own.

And that is the purpose of this little book. I want to take these tantalizing messages from the pen of Luke, inspired by the Holy Spirit, and construct for myself and for my readers scriptural proof that Jesus is the Christ and that his coming and, more importantly, his sacrifice and death, were prophesied of old. Indeed, I believe it is just this mystery that Paul referred to when he tells us that God's plan of salvation is a "mystery . . . kept hidden for ages and generations" (Col 1:26 NIV; see also Eph 3:9–12). And thus the title of this little book, *The Mystery Kept Hidden for Ages and Generations*. Within this book we will begin the process of uncovering that mystery and recovering the Old Testament proof that spilled from the lips of Jesus, Paul, and Apollos. We begin the process here, and for each of my readers the process is completed as they digest what I say and add their own proofs from their own scriptural study and analysis.

2.

The Weeks in Scripture

IT IS SAID ONE cannot prove the existence of God; instead God's existence must be accepted on faith or not at all. In this section, however, I offer what I believe to be a strong argument for God's existence and for the truth of the Judaeo-Christian worldview, an argument based only in part on faith but mostly on empirical proof. In other words, if the principles offered here are accepted by the reader, then we have constructed a logical argument for the existence of the God of Scripture, and we've done so by seemingly irrefutable logic.

This is dynamic.

Let me explain and provide background. I have long been aware of two weeks in the scriptural account, weeks of central interest to Bible readers. I have recently become aware of a third week, and I think there is an interesting relationship between the three that God may have hidden within the text as part of his mystery kept hidden for ages and generations. And perhaps they are part of the proof adduced by Jesus, Paul, and Apollos to prove the truth of God's plan of salvation.

The first week of which even the most casual of Bible readers will be aware is the week of creation found in Genesis, chapter 1. According to that passage, God created the universe in a six-day work week and rested on the seventh day. The passage has intrigued readers and inflamed passions. The literalists among us contend it establishes beyond dispute that God created the universe in a short seven days. Based upon this premise, they reject the concept of evolution and are somewhat mystified by the archeological and geological record that establishes both a very old universe and an astonishing period of time between the first creation and the appearance of man.

The less literal among us believe that Gen 1 and 2 were intended for its Jewish audience to explain that the God whom they worshipped, the God who redeemed them from Egyptian bondage, is the one God who created the universe. To Moses and to God, it is imperatively important that the Hebrews, recently freed from slavery in Egypt, know that this amazing force that caused Egypt, then the most powerful nation on earth, to release them from enslavement is the great God of creation. Powerful Egypt's economy, wholly dependent upon the massive free labor of its Jewish slaves, bowed to the great force of a God the Jews had heard of only heretofore in family discussions and ancient stories retold around campfires. And the great deed, emancipation, occurred without the powerless Jews "firing a shot" or raising a hand in violence. Who was this God who defeated Egypt for them? The book of Genesis, and its creation story, are intended to answer that very vital question. Then as now, God is progressively revealing himself to his people—here, the Jews—and, having displayed his power over the most powerful nation on earth, it is now his intention to share with them his role in creation.

For those of us who embrace this view, the characterization of the creation process as a seven-day event is mystifying, but it is not intended to establish the chronological duration of the creation process. That raises the question, however, why did the author, perhaps Moses, craft his narrative as a seven-day creation event? Even more importantly, why did God inspire the author to describe creation as occurring in a mere seven days? To me the purpose of the Genesis creation narrative is to tie the Creator to the Redeemer, he who broke the will of Egypt. The purpose is not to establish scientifically, to Darwin's chagrin, that creation took only a week. There must, instead, be another reason for truncating the story of creation. If, as I believe, Gen 1–2 is not a science text but a self-revelation by the one and only God, that is, "I AM the Creator and Redeemer," why did he choose to describe creation as a one-week project? These are questions to which we will return.

Creation week, then, is the first of two weeks in Scripture that stand out even to the most casual of Bible readers.

The second week in Scripture, well known to the student of the Bible, is the passion week, the week that climaxes the Four Gospels and forms the centerpiece of the New Testament in Christian theology. Passion week, actually an eight-day narration, encompasses two Sundays. It begins with Palm Sunday, Jesus's triumphal entry into Jerusalem, one week before Easter Sunday, and it ends on that Easter Sunday when even more triumphantly Jesus returns to life from a Jerusalem tomb, defeating death and Satan, and inspiring even remaking the world. The Gospel passages provide significant information concerning Jesus's activities during that week in Jerusalem, a week that began with a "ticker tape parade" celebrating the great prophet who had raised Lazarus from the dead a few weeks before, plummeting thereafter to the terrible crucifixion of Friday, when the great hero of Palm Sunday was ridiculed, spat upon, and crucified with all the barbarity that hideous crucifixion entailed. Then, the roller coaster of passion week concludes with the triumphant Easter Sunday when the sacrificed Christ rises from the dead. Not since the amazing week of creation has history seen such a week as passion week.

Might there be a reason, a connection, between these weeks, cryptically included in the Bible, the great narrative of God's romance with mankind? Creation week and passion week appear unrelated. But might that be untrue? Might there be a connection? In fact, might creation be recounted in a brief week so that readers like us, thousands of years later, would be drawn to passion week for comparisons? After all, he whom John told us spoke creation into existence is the same one who endures passion week and proclaims in Revelation that he is "making all things new" (Rev 21:5 NRSV; cf. Gen 1 and John 1).That is, he, Jesus, is creating all over again, "making all things new."

I recently learned that a third week exists in Scripture and it caused me to suspect a connection between creation week and passion week and, within that connection, to suspect another hint to the mystery kept hidden for ages and generations. I became aware of that third week when, in a study of the Psalms, I learned that, after the Jewish remnant returned from Babylon at the end of captivity, and after rededicating the rebuilt temple in Jerusalem, approximately 500 BC, Jewish priests delved into the Psalter to select seven psalms (hymns) to compose a weekly liturgy of worship. Within this framework, the priests assigned a specific song to each day of the week. From that selection forward, each day in the temple had a specific psalm assigned to it, a psalm that had special meaning to its author, to its audience, and to us. The psalm of the day pattern repeated itself throughout the life of the temple, ending presumably in AD 70, when Rome destroyed the temple. According to John Phillips, in *Exploring the Psalms*, the chosen songs align as follows: for Sunday, Ps 24; for Monday, Ps 48; for Tuesday, Ps 82; for Wednesday, Ps. 94; for Thursday, Ps 81; for Friday, Ps 93; and for Saturday, Ps 92.[1]

As I studied these psalms, I saw what I thought to be a direct relationship between the psalm assigned to a day of the week and the events of passion week on that day of the week. In other words, the psalm for Sunday appeared to connect with the events of Palm Sunday and Easter Sunday, and so forth. This will be developed more below. Thereafter, while attempting to analyze the peculiar relationship between those psalms and the days of passion week, I became further aware that one could similarly identify elements from each day of creation that corresponded to the song of the day and surprisingly to the corresponding day of passion week as well. In other words, there seemed to be a relationship between the psalm of the day, selected by the priests circa 500 BC, and both

1. Phillips, *Exploring the Psalms*, 1:180.

the corresponding events of that same day in creation week and in passion week. Because creation week was clearly in the past for the postexilic Jews and the priests who assigned psalms to days of the week, that realization was surprising but not shocking. Knowing what Gen 1 said happened on each day of creation week, the priests could make a conscious choice of which psalm best suited the creation narrative. In fact, that is precisely what the priests did. In selecting the psalms of the day, what they called *Shir shel yom*, those priests tried to select songs that bore some relationship to that appropriate day of creation, as Gen 1 describes those days.[2] But because for those priests the events of passion week were five hundred years in the future, my surprise grew to shock. Unless guided by the hand (better perhaps the Word) of God, those priests could never have anticipated that their choices would mirror the events of passion week. Indeed, the psalms selected seemed to fit the events of passion week, five hundred years in the future, better, much better, than they fit the days of creation.

This realization was exciting. In the passages and analyses below, we will go day by day through the days of the week, look at the events of creation week to see what creation tasks were accomplished in that given day, compare those events to the psalm of the day, and look to see if each foreshadowed the events of that same day in the chronology of passion week. Clearly, to the extent that there is a relationship between those two literary phenomena and the priestly choices of daily psalms, written and acted out over several millennia, it suggests that a singular intelligence arranged the seeming serendipity. Just as clearly, there is no single individual human intelligence that lived through the creation, the temple worship in the Second Temple period and the roller coaster events of passion week. If there is a unifying theme overarching these primeval eons, who can be its author? No detractor or doubter can come face to face with the parallel similarities of these three weeks in Scripture, separated by eons, without recognizing that behind it all there is one magnificent intelligence, and it can only be YHWH, the great I AM, the one true God.

2. Apple, "Psalms of the Day."

And now, with the psalms of the day thrown into the discussion, let me return to the question posed earlier. Might there be a reason, a connection, between these weeks, cryptically included in the Bible, the great narrative of God's romance with mankind? Creation week, passion week, and the psalms of the day appear unrelated. But might that be untrue? Are there connections? And, if connections exist, what does that mean? What does it say to us as believers? And, more importantly, what does it say to nonbelievers? How can the skeptical respond?

Below, then, we will take each day of the week in order. We will enumerate the events of creation week; we will do the same for that day in passion week; and we will analyze the psalm of the day to see what, if anything, it says about the corresponding days of creation week and passion week. If there be parallels, one can only conclude that there is one author.

And, if there be one author, our faith must be accepted, not on faith but on proof.

Proof!

For only God can be that one author.

3.

The First Day (Sunday)

ON SUNDAY, THE FIRST day of creation week, Gen 1 tells us succinctly,

> In the beginning God created the heaven and the earth. And the earth was without form, and void; and darkness was upon the face of the deep. And the Spirit of God moved upon the face of the waters. And God said, Let there be light: and there was light. And God saw the light, that it was good: and God divided the light from the darkness. And God called the light Day, and the darkness he called Night. And the evening and the morning were the first day. (vv. 1–5)

Per Gen 1, then, on the first day of creation, Sunday, God created day and night, speaking them into existence, an event accomplished through the introduction of light. The entry of light demands additional thought.

In the Gospel of John, we learn new information about creation, at least three things that bear upon Monday of creation. First, John tells us that the Christ is that aspect of the triune God which performed creation. Says John,

> In the beginning was the Word, and the Word was with God, and the Word was God. The same was in the

beginning with God. All things were made by him; and without him was not any thing made that was made. (John 1:1–3)

That same passage also calls the Christ the Word, meaning, I think, that when God (the Christ, in fact) speaks the universe into existence, it is done by way of his Word, the Christ. As Genesis says, read in the context of John 1, God (the Father) speaks his Word (the Son, the Christ) and creation occurs.

The third fact revealed by John is that Christ is also the Light, the same light perhaps which enters into creation and by which day and night are divided. Says John,

> In him was life; and the life was the light of men. And the light shineth in darkness; and the darkness comprehended it not. There was a man sent from God, whose name was John. The same came for a witness, to bear witness of the Light, that all men through him might believe. He was not that Light, but was sent to bear witness of that Light. That was the true Light, which lighteth every man that cometh into the world. (John 1:4–9)

These then are the events of the first day of creation, as amplified by the Gospel of John. Jesus, the Christ, created day and night. Jesus, the Light, divided day from night. And Jesus, the Word, spoke all this into existence. In effect, the Christ, the Word, the Light entered into the void that existed before creation dawned.

Our next task is to recount the events of the first Sunday of passion week, but first another aspect of creation bears noting, that is, creation must be repeated. Remember John identifies the preincarnate Christ as the aspect of God's personality responsible for creation. Christ, the Word, spoke creation into existence. Paul tells us the same (Col 1:15–20). But after creation, mankind then sins (Gen 3), and the curse of that sin falls upon God's creation, effectively spoiling it. That must be remedied, and only God can do that.

God's remedy lies in the sacrifice of self by Jesus and his subsequent resurrection. In effect, the Christ who initially created must create again, removing the curse of sin and reversing the spoil. Thus in Revelation, Jesus proclaims, I am making all things new! (Rev 21:5 NRSV). That means, of course, that the Creator Christ is fulfilling his role of recreating the perfect creation that resulted from his efforts in Gen 1. He must make all things new because no one else can do it. Jesus must do it because, as his forebear David said in a psalm prophetic of the crucifixion, "I am forced to restore what I did not steal" (Ps 69:4b NIV). That is precisely what Jesus is doing as he proclaims, "I am making all things new!" Jesus is making all things new, restoring what he did not steal.

The upshot is this: Regardless of whether my premise proves true, whether there be direct correlation between the psalms of the day and the events of passion week, there is one overarching parallel between creation week and passion week. In both "weeks," the Christ is creating; first in Gen 1 and then again in the Gospels, he "is making all things new."

With that, we now turn to passion week.

The events of the first Sunday of passion week, Palm Sunday, appear in the Synoptic Gospels:

> And when they drew nigh unto Jerusalem, and were come to Bethphage, unto the mount of Olives, then sent Jesus two disciples, Saying unto them, Go into the village over against you, and straightway ye shall find an ass tied, and a colt with her: loose them, and bring them unto me. And if any man say ought unto you, ye shall say, The Lord hath need of them; and straightway he will send them. All this was done, that it might be fulfilled which was spoken by the prophet, saying, Tell ye the daughter of Sion, Behold, thy King cometh unto thee, meek, and sitting upon an ass, and a colt the foal of an ass. And the disciples went, and did as Jesus commanded them, And brought the ass, and the colt, and put on them their clothes, and they set him thereon. And a very great multitude spread their garments in the way; others cut down branches from the trees, and strawed them in the way. And the multitudes that went before, and that followed, cried, saying, Hosanna to the son of David: Blessed is

he that cometh in the name of the Lord; Hosanna in the highest. And when he was come into Jerusalem, all the city was moved, saying, Who is this? And the multitude said, This is Jesus the prophet of Nazareth of Galilee. (Matt 21:1–11)

Matthew here tells us that, on the first Sunday of passion week, Palm Sunday, Jesus entered into Jerusalem to the loud acclaim of the Jewish people, gathered there for the Passover Feast in the week to come. The excitement arose from Jesus's fame as a prophet; the burgeoning crowds thought him the messiah himself; and the raising of Lazarus mere weeks before (John 11) fanned both the fervor of the crowd and the furor of the temple rulers.

On Palm Sunday, the first day of passion week, Jesus entered into Jerusalem. And, once there, the great dance of redemption began. That bears repeating: on Palm Sunday, Jesus entered into Jerusalem.

Now let us see what the psalm of the day for Sunday tells us.

The psalm of the day for Sunday, selected by the Jewish priests in approximately 500 BC, was Ps 24.

Psalm 24 is a psalm of David, written by the shepherd king to celebrate a very special event in the history of the Jewish people. In the psalm, David memorializes the glorious day on which he succeeded in bringing into Jerusalem, into his new capital, the ark of the covenant.

A little context sets the stage.

The ark was tooled by the Israelites at the foot of Mount Sinai per the strict instructions of God to Moses, instructions delivered to Moses at about the same time that Moses received the Ten Commandments (Exod 25:8–22). From that moment forward, the ark represented the presence of God himself. It was constructed, in fact, in God's own words, "so that I may live among them"—that is, among God's people (Exod 25:8).

This is important: the ark represents, even *is* to the Jews, the presence of God himself. God says so himself.

It is no surprise, then, that the ark wields great power among the Israelites, their friends, and their enemies. It leads them as they wander in the wilderness (Num 10:33–36). When the people pleased God, acted within God's will and wishes, the ark brought them success on the battlefield (Num 14:39–45). When the people displeased God, the ark, God's presence, could bring them military failure (1 Sam 4). But the ark was always anathema to Israel's enemies whether accompanied by Jewish battlefield success or not (1 Sam 4:1—7:2).

Much of the ark's history, and how it figured in David's authorship of Ps 24, is recorded in 1 Sam 4:1—7:2 and in 2 Sam 6:1–19. The story runs that Israel tried to use the ark for military advantage even as they failed to do God's will, leading to a predictable result. Though the entry of the ark into the Israelite camp led nervous Philistine soldiers to venture that "God has come into" the Israelite camp, Israel fell to the Philistines that day, and the ark was captured (1 Sam 4:7–11).

Thereafter, the ark bedeviled its Philistine captors. It humiliated the pagan god Dagon and struck the Philistines with scourges of mice and tumors. Finally, the Philistines tired of the unbeatable forces the ark loosed upon them, and they allowed the ark, pulled by meandering milk cows, to wind its way back into Israel. Once back in Israel, the ark remained for twenty years in nondescript villages outside the capital of the nation.

But after David became king and captured his new capital, Jerusalem, he yearned to bring the ark, representing the presence and the dwelling of God, into his capital city. David wanted the ark in Jerusalem. But the introduction of the ark into Jerusalem did not occur without hiccup. When David first attempted it, the procession loaded the ark onto a cart and started the journey. Along the way, though, the cart became unsettled, the ark trembled and an attendant, Uzzah, reached out to settle it. Instantly, Uzzah fell dead.

With this disastrous development, David reconsidered his plan to bring the ark into Jerusalem. Instead, he lodged it in the "house of Obed-edom, the Gittite" (2 Sam 6:10 NRSV). There it stayed for three months until positive reports caused David to try yet again to bring the ark, the presence of the Lord, into Jerusalem.

This time David's efforts succeeded. The ark, the presence of the Lord, reached Jerusalem, and was placed in the home David prepared for it. And David rejoiced, dancing to such a fervor that his wife, Michal, daughter of former King Saul, became so embarrassed that she "despised [David] in her heart . . . and had no child to the day of her death" (2 Sam 6:1–19).

But that is not the end of the story. David was so exhilarated at bringing God's lodging, God's very presence, into Jerusalem that David penned Ps 24 to memorialize the portentous event. This is what David wrote:

> The earth is the LORD's, and the fulness thereof; the world, and they that dwell therein.
>
> For he hath founded it upon the seas, and established it upon the floods.
>
> Who shall ascend into the hill of the LORD? or who shall stand in his holy place?
>
> He that hath clean hands, and a pure heart; who hath not lifted up his soul unto vanity, nor sworn deceitfully.
>
> He shall receive the blessing from the LORD, and righteousness from the God of his salvation.
>
> This is the generation of them that seek him, that seek thy face, O Jacob. Selah.
>
> Lift up your heads, O ye gates; and be ye lifted up, ye everlasting doors; and the King of glory shall come in. Who is this King of glory? The LORD strong and mighty, the LORD mighty in battle.
>
> Lift up your heads, O ye gates; even lift them up, ye everlasting doors; and the King of glory shall come in.
>
> Who is this King of glory? The LORD of hosts, he is the King of glory. Selah.

The ark, God's very presence, entered into Jerusalem and to celebrate David wrote Ps 24, the future psalm of Sunday, the first day of the week.

So, to summarize:

1. On the first day of creation week, the Christ, the Word, the light, entered into the void that existed before creation dawned.

2. On Palm Sunday, the first day of passion week, Jesus, the Christ, God himself, entered into Jerusalem.

3. In the psalm of the day for Sunday, the first day of the week, Ps 24, David celebrated the fact that the ark, the presence of God, entered into Jerusalem.

4. The parallels are clear: each day features the entry of God himself into creation or into the city of David, Jerusalem.

5. Because the psalm of the day for Sunday, Ps 24, was selected for that day five hundred years before the birth of Jesus, we have either great serendipity or the hand of God selecting the psalm.

In sum, as to the psalm of the day and Palm Sunday, the overriding theme of each is God entering Jerusalem whether emblematic in the ark of the covenant or in the very person of Jesus, God made man.

And nothing can better describe Jesus's entry into Jerusalem on Palm Sunday than David's words penned one thousand years before and selected for Sunday five hundred years thereafter.

> Lift up your heads, O ye gates; and be ye lifted up, ye everlasting doors; and the King of glory shall come in.
>
> Who is this King of glory? The LORD strong and mighty, the LORD mighty in battle.
>
> Lift up your heads, O ye gates; even lift them up, ye everlasting doors; and the King of glory shall come in.
>
> Who is this King of glory? The LORD of hosts, he is the King of glory. (Ps 24:7–10).

Though written and selected centuries before passion week, these words of David describe the events of Palm Sunday better than any description found in the gospels. If that be intentional, then only one intelligence could have made the selection.

4.

The Second Day (Monday)

On Monday, the second day of creation week, Gen 1 says,

> And God said, Let there be a firmament in the midst of
> the waters, and let it divide the waters from the waters.
> And God made the firmament, and divided the waters
> which were under the firmament from the waters which
> were above the firmament: and it was so. And God called
> the firmament Heaven. And the evening and the morn-
> ing were the second day. (vv. 6–8)

Genesis 1 says, then, that on the second day of creation God created heaven. The King James Version uses the term "heaven"; some
versions use the term "sky." Either way, and however one wants to
interpret "heaven," the clear meaning is the sky above our heads.
But it is indisputable that for ancient mankind, and many moderns
today, the heavens above and the sky itself are thought to be the
dwelling place of God. Indeed, as late as the first century AD, New
Testament author Luke, who produced both the Gospel of Luke
and the Acts of the Apostles, perceived the skies above as heaven
and the locus of the living God. In Luke 24:50–51, Luke tells us
that Jesus ascended into heaven. In Acts 1:9–11, Luke repeats the
claim with some elaboration:

> And when he had spoken these things, while they beheld, he was taken up; and a cloud received him out of their sight. And while they looked steadfastly toward heaven as he went up, behold, two men stood by them in white apparel; Which also said, Ye men of Galilee, why stand ye gazing up into heaven? this same Jesus, which is taken up from you into heaven, shall so come in like manner as ye have seen him go into heaven.

Furthermore, Luke describes the stoning of Christian martyr Stephen, concluding by describing Stephen peering up into heaven just before death, seeing there Jesus at the right hand of God, the Father:

> When they heard these things, they were cut to the heart, and they gnashed on him with their teeth. But he [Stephen], being full of the Holy Ghost, looked up stedfastly into heaven, and saw the glory of God, and Jesus standing on the right hand of God, And said, Behold, I see the heavens opened, and the Son of man standing on the right hand of God. (Acts 7:54–56)

In both instances, Luke and his audience viewed the heavens—heaven, if you will—as the dwelling place of God.

Consequently, the second day of creation in the creation narrative of Gen 1 can be seen as God creating heaven, which mankind justifiably or not will come to view as God's home.

But to God's chosen people, the Jews, a different and more localized dwelling for Jehovah is needed. Thus, at Sinai, under the leadership of Moses, God shares with the Jews a detailed design for an artifact that he will allow the Jews to use as a representative of his divine presence, the locus at which he may be found in their midst (Exod 25:8–22). The ark of the covenant becomes, in effect, God's dwelling place among the itinerant Jews, supplanting the heavens.

But the story continues: The ark becomes for the Jews the dwelling place of God as they wander through the wilderness of Sinai, and that does not change after they reach the promised land. In fact, the ark maintains that status into the era of Jewish kings, and is not replaced until Solomon, son of David, builds the temple in Jerusalem. Only then does the dwelling place of God, that physical representation of his presence, shift from the ark to the temple. As Solomon dedicates the temple in an ornate service, the Shekinah of God settles into the newly built temple, and the temple becomes God's house (2 Sam 7:1–13; 1 Chr 22:1–2, 5–11; Ps 74:2–7). Speaking of the temple, God himself says, "My house shall be called a house of prayer . . . but you have made it a den of robbers" (Isa 56:7; Jer 7:11; Mark 11:17).

To summarize, on the second day of creation in Gen 1, God creates his dwelling place, heaven. Then, over time in God's relationship with the Jews, that dwelling place becomes more localized, first with the ark of the covenant and thereafter in Jerusalem and the temple.

The events of the second day of passion week are, of course, described in the Synoptic Gospels:

> And on the morrow . . . they come to Jerusalem: and Jesus went into the temple, and began to cast out them that sold and bought in the temple, and overthrew the tables of the moneychangers, and the seats of them that sold doves; And would not suffer that any man should carry any vessel through the temple. And he taught, saying unto them, Is it not written, My house shall be called of all nations the house of prayer? but ye have made it a den of thieves. And the scribes and chief priests heard it, and sought how they might destroy him: for they feared him, because all the people was astonished at his doctrine. And when even was come, he went out of the city. (Mark 11:12, 15–19)

Thus, on the second day (Monday) of passion week, Jesus defends the honor of the temple, God's house, his dwelling place, and ejects the Passover money changers who are defrauding the worshippers who have come to Jerusalem and to the temple to celebrate the holy Passover Feast.

Comparing creation week with passion week, we see a vague correlation. In creation week on this the second day, God creates heaven in which, in man's mind, God will dwell. And in subsequent times that dwelling place becomes, first, the ark and, thereafter, the temple. Then on this second day of passion week Jesus defends the temple, that place that God calls "my house," and ejects the moneychangers whose conduct defiles the holy premises. In sum, God creates his dwelling place, and Jesus defends God's dwelling place.

Now we turn to the psalm of the day for Monday, the second day of the week, remembering that these psalms were chosen for these days five hundred years before the birth of Jesus. That psalm is Ps 48.

Psalm 48 was written, it is believed, by either Isaiah or by King Hezekiah, who were contemporaries. The events that triggered Ps 48 are remarkable, so much so that they are described in several Old Testament sources. Two chapters in 2 Kings cover the event (chs. 18–19), as does one chapter in 2 Chronicles (ch. 32) and two chapters in Isaiah (chs. 36–37).

The approximate date was 701 BC. Hezekiah is Judah's king, and Isaiah is active as God's prophet. Hezekiah is one of Judah's best, most righteous, kings (see 2 Chr 29–31). And Isaiah is one of the Old Testament's major prophets. Thus, Judah is in good hands, and, given the crisis to come, that is a very good thing.

The adversary is Assyria, the bane of the Old Testament, whom some would call the Third Reich of ancient times, comparing them to Nazi Germany. The Assyrians were bombastic and brutal.

Some Assyrian history is beneficial here. A little over a century before, Assyria had overrun the Northern Kingdom, Israel, and removed the ruling classes of Jews from that nation, replacing them with the immigrants who intermarried with the local Jews (2 Kings 17:24–41). The peoples who resulted from this social unrest become the Samaritans of the New Testament.

Now, in Hezekiah's time, Assyria remains aggressive, and having subjugated Israel, they set their sights upon Judah. Scripture tells us that the Assyrians under their King Sennacherib invade Judah and capture "all the fortified cities of Judah," except for Jerusalem (2 Kgs 18:13). Then, despite Hezekiah's efforts to appease Sennacherib, a "great army" of Assyrians proceeds to the walls of Jerusalem, where their commander, Rabshakeh, insults and threatens in turn the city itself, King Hezekiah, and "this altar in Jerusalem," that is, the temple (2 Kgs 18:13–25). Rabshakeh, when asked to speak only to Hezekiah's representatives so as not to frighten the populace, profanely pronounces that the populace should hear what he says because they will soon be forced "to eat their own dung and drink their own urine" (2 Kgs 18:27 NRSV).

The Assyrian reputation for barbarity, you can see, is well deserved.

Rabshakeh's threats are communicated to Hezekiah, and the King of Judah, whose domain has been stripped of its fortified cities and who sees a vast army arrayed before his capital, tears his clothing in dismay. Then he "went into the house of the Lord" (2 Kgs 19:1). In other words, Hezekiah retreats to the dwelling place of God, to the temple. Hezekiah dispatches ministers to confer with Isaiah, the prophet, and the drama deepens. Rabshakeh sends Hezekiah yet another message, and finally, Hezekiah returns to the temple, the house of the Lord, to share the crisis with God Almighty:

> And Hezekiah received the letter of the hand of the messengers, and read it: and Hezekiah went up into the house of the LORD, and spread it before the LORD. And Hezekiah prayed before the LORD, and said, O LORD God of Israel, which dwellest between the cherubims, thou art the God, even thou alone, of all the kingdoms of the earth; thou hast made heaven and earth. LORD, bow down thine ear, and hear: open, LORD, thine eyes, and see: and hear the words of Sennacherib, which hath sent him to reproach the living God. Of a truth, LORD, the kings of Assyria have destroyed the nations and their lands, And have cast their gods into the fire: for they were no gods, but the work of men's hands, wood and stone: therefore they have destroyed them. Now therefore, O

> LORD our God, I beseech thee, save thou us out of his
> hand, that all the kingdoms of the earth may know that
> thou art the LORD God, even thou only. Then Isaiah the
> son of Amoz sent to Hezekiah, saying, Thus saith the
> LORD God of Israel, That which thou hast prayed to me
> against Sennacherib king of Assyria I have heard. This
> is the word that the LORD hath spoken concerning him.
> ... Therefore thus saith the LORD concerning the king of
> Assyria, He shall not come into this city, nor shoot an ar-
> row there, nor come before it with shield, nor cast a bank
> against it. By the way that he came, by the same shall he
> return, and shall not come into this city, saith the LORD.
> For I will defend this city, to save it, for mine own sake,
> and for my servant David's sake. And it came to pass that
> night, that the angel of the LORD went out, and smote
> in the camp of the Assyrians an hundred fourscore and
> five thousand: and when they arose early in the morning,
> behold, they were all dead corpses. So Sennacherib king
> of Assyria departed, and went and returned, and dwelt at
> Nineveh. (2 Kgs 19:14–21, 32–36)

It bears noting that the Scripture records the temple as the "house
of the Lord" and that Hezekiah in his prayer says that God "dwell-
est between the cherubims," which appears to refer to the ark that
presumably sat in the naos of the temple. It is Jerusalem and the
temple that God pledges to defend he does defend. In fact, the
angel of the Lord moves miraculously among the Assyrian army
that night, and in the morning there are 185,000 dead Assyrian
soldiers, the handiwork of the angel of the Lord, as he defends the
dwelling place of God—that is, Jerusalem and its temple.

These are the events that Ps 48 celebrates. The miraculous
defeat of Sennacherib's Assyrians by the Old Testament angel of
the Lord (thought by many to be the preincarnate Christ) ranks
with the defeat of Egypt and the splitting of the Red Sea as God's
greatest works to defend Israel. All the cities of Judah, save Jerusalem, had been captured; the situation was hopeless. But God
intervened and God alone defended his city, his home, his temple.

And here is Ps 48, written most likely by Hezekiah or Isaiah, to celebrate God's defense of God's house, the temple, and his city, Jerusalem.

> Great is the LORD, and greatly to be praised in the city of our God, in the mountain of his holiness.
>
> Beautiful for situation, the joy of the whole earth, is mount Zion, on the sides of the north, the city of the great King.
>
> God is known in her palaces for a refuge.
>
> For, lo, the kings were assembled, they passed by together.
>
> They saw it, and so they marvelled; they were troubled, and hasted away.
>
> Fear took hold upon them there, and pain, as of a woman in travail.
>
> Thou breakest the ships of Tarshish with an east wind.
>
> As we have heard, so have we seen in the city of the LORD of hosts, in the city of our God: God will establish it for ever. Selah.
>
> We have thought of thy lovingkindness, O God, in the midst of thy temple.
>
> According to thy name, O God, so is thy praise unto the ends of the earth: thy right hand is full of righteousness.
>
> Let mount Zion rejoice, let the daughters of Judah be glad, because of thy judgments.
>
> Walk about Zion, and go round about her: tell the towers thereof.
>
> Mark ye well her bulwarks, consider her palaces; that ye may tell it to the generation following.
>
> For this God is our God for ever and ever: he will be our guide even unto death.

So, to summarize:

1. On the second day of creation week, Monday, God (the Christ, the Word) creates the sky, the heavens, long considered by men to be the dwelling of God.

2. On the second day of passion week, Monday, Jesus, God incarnate, cleanses—defends—the temple, the dwelling place of God ("My house shall be a house of prayer").

3. In the Monday psalm, Ps 48, Isaiah and/or Hezekiah celebrate God's (the angel of the Lord's, that is, Christ's) defense of God's dwelling place, Jerusalem and the temple.

As with day one, the passages for day two are linked, each addressing the creating, defending, and cleansing of the dwelling place of God. So far, then, the premise holds. There is correlation between the days in the week of creation, the same days in passion week, and the psalms or hymns of the day selected by the priests five hundred years before the birth of Jesus.

And, if the premise holds true as we progress through this exercise, we will have proven that God selected the hymns knowing what God's plan of salvation would entail five hundred years later. No Jewish priest could have selected such content-appropriate psalms five hundred years before the events of passion week. God himself must have made the selections.

In other words, we will have proven the Christian faith. It is true.

5.

The Third Day (Tuesday)

ON TUESDAY, THE THIRD day of creation week, Gen 1 tells us:

> And God said, Let the waters under the heaven be gathered together unto one place, and let the dry land appear: and it was so. And God called the dry land Earth; and the gathering together of the waters called the Seas: and God saw that it was good. And God said, Let the earth bring forth grass, the herb yielding seed, and the fruit tree yielding fruit after his kind, whose seed is in itself, upon the earth: and it was so. And the earth brought forth grass, and herb yielding seed after his kind, and the tree yielding fruit, whose seed was in itself, after his kind: and God saw that it was good. And the evening and the morning were the third day. (vv. 9–13)

Per Gen 1, then, on the third day of creation, Tuesday, God created the dry land, the Earth, and the wet, the seas. Furthermore, God commanded the Earth to yield plant life, fruit, and seeds. By the act of creation and by ordering reproduction via seeds and seedlings, God effectively exercised his dominion over Earth.

The events of Tuesday of passion week are voluminous. Tuesday of passion week is commonly called the Day of Controversy, the day on which the temple authorities posed rapid fire questions, most of them tricky, and all intended to transform the hero of Palm Sunday's "ticker tape parade" into Good Friday's abandoned victim. The Synoptic Gospels each devote considerable space and verbiage to the Day of Controversy. Those passages are: Matt 21:18—26:25, Mark 11:20—13:37, and Luke 19:47—21:38.

Matthew's account is the most extensive, and it contains at least two questions and answers that are not found in Mark or Luke. Here are the pertinent portions of Matthew's account of Tuesday of passion week:

> Now in the morning as he returned into the city. . . .
>
> And when he was come into the temple, the chief priests and the elders of the people came unto him as he was teaching, and said, By what authority doest thou these things? and who gave thee this authority?
>
> And Jesus answered and said unto them, I also will ask you one thing, which if ye tell me, I in like wise will tell you by what authority I do these things.
>
> The baptism of John, whence was it? from heaven, or of men? And they reasoned with themselves, saying, If we shall say, From heaven; he will say unto us, Why did ye not then believe him?
>
> But if we shall say, Of men; we fear the people; for all hold John as a prophet.
>
> And they answered Jesus, and said, We cannot tell. And he said unto them, Neither tell I you by what authority I do these things.
>
> But what think ye? A certain man had two sons; and he came to the first, and said, Son, go work to day in my vineyard.
>
> He answered and said, I will not: but afterward he repented, and went.
>
> And he came to the second, and said likewise. And he answered and said, I go, sir: and went not.
>
> Whether of them twain did the will of his father? They say unto him, The first. Jesus saith unto them, Verily I say unto you, That the publicans and the harlots go into the kingdom of God before you.

For John came unto you in the way of righteousness, and ye believed him not: but the publicans and the harlots believed him: and ye, when ye had seen it, repented not afterward, that ye might believe him.

Hear another parable: There was a certain householder, which planted a vineyard, and hedged it round about, and digged a winepress in it, and built a tower, and let it out to husbandmen, and went into a far country:

And when the time of the fruit drew near, he sent his servants to the husbandmen, that they might receive the fruits of it.

And the husbandmen took his servants, and beat one, and killed another, and stoned another.

Again, he sent other servants more than the first: and they did unto them likewise.

But last of all he sent unto them his son, saying, They will reverence my son.

But when the husbandmen saw the son, they said among themselves, This is the heir; come, let us kill him, and let us seize on his inheritance.

And they caught him, and cast him out of the vineyard, and slew him.

When the lord therefore of the vineyard cometh, what will he do unto those husbandmen?

They say unto him, He will miserably destroy those wicked men, and will let out his vineyard unto other husbandmen, which shall render him the fruits in their seasons.

Jesus saith unto them, Did ye never read in the scriptures, The stone which the builders rejected, the same is become the head of the corner: this is the Lord's doing, and it is marvellous in our eyes?

Therefore say I unto you, The kingdom of God shall be taken from you, and given to a nation bringing forth the fruits thereof.

And whosoever shall fall on this stone shall be broken: but on whomsoever it shall fall, it will grind him to powder.

And when the chief priests and Pharisees had heard his parables, they perceived that he spake of them.

But when they sought to lay hands on him, they feared the multitude, because they took him for a prophet.

And Jesus answered and spake unto them again by parables, and said,

The kingdom of heaven is like unto a certain king, which made a marriage for his son,

And sent forth his servants to call them that were bidden to the wedding: and they would not come.

Again, he sent forth other servants, saying, Tell them which are bidden, Behold, I have prepared my dinner: my oxen and my fatlings are killed, and all things are ready: come unto the marriage.

But they made light of it, and went their ways, one to his farm, another to his merchandise:

And the remnant took his servants, and entreated them spitefully, and slew them.

But when the king heard thereof, he was wroth: and he sent forth his armies, and destroyed those murderers, and burned up their city.

Then saith he to his servants, The wedding is ready, but they which were bidden were not worthy.

Go ye therefore into the highways, and as many as ye shall find, bid to the marriage.

So those servants went out into the highways, and gathered together all as many as they found, both bad and good: and the wedding was furnished with guests.

And when the king came in to see the guests, he saw there a man which had not on a wedding garment:

And he saith unto him, Friend, how camest thou in hither not having a wedding garment? And he was speechless.

Then said the king to the servants, Bind him hand and foot, and take him away, and cast him into outer darkness, there shall be weeping and gnashing of teeth.

For many are called, but few are chosen.

Then went the Pharisees, and took counsel how they might entangle him in his talk.

And they sent out unto him their disciples with the Herodians, saying, Master, we know that thou art true, and teachest the way of God in truth, neither carest thou for any man: for thou regardest not the person of men.

Tell us therefore, What thinkest thou? Is it lawful to give tribute unto Caesar, or not?

But Jesus perceived their wickedness, and said, Why tempt ye me, ye hypocrites?

Shew me the tribute money. And they brought unto him a penny.

And he saith unto them, Whose is this image and superscription?

They say unto him, Caesar's. Then saith he unto them, Render therefore unto Caesar the things which are Caesar's; and unto God the things that are God's.

When they had heard these words, they marvelled, and left him, and went their way.

The same day came to him the Sadducees, which say that there is no resurrection, and asked him,

Saying, Master, Moses said, If a man die, having no children, his brother shall marry his wife, and raise up seed unto his brother.

Now there were with us seven brethren: and the first, when he had married a wife, deceased, and, having no issue, left his wife unto his brother:

Likewise the second also, and the third, unto the seventh.

And last of all the woman died also.

Therefore in the resurrection whose wife shall she be of the seven? for they all had her.

Jesus answered and said unto them, Ye do err, not knowing the scriptures, nor the power of God.

For in the resurrection they neither marry, nor are given in marriage, but are as the angels of God in heaven.

But as touching the resurrection of the dead, have ye not read that which was spoken unto you by God, saying,

I am the God of Abraham, and the God of Isaac, and the God of Jacob? God is not the God of the dead, but of the living.

And when the multitude heard this, they were astonished at his doctrine.

But when the Pharisees had heard that he had put the Sadducees to silence, they were gathered together.

Then one of them, which was a lawyer, asked him a question, tempting him, and saying,

Master, which is the great commandment in the law?

Jesus said unto him, Thou shalt love the Lord thy God with all thy heart, and with all thy soul, and with all thy mind.

This is the first and great commandment.

And the second is like unto it, Thou shalt love thy neighbour as thyself.

On these two commandments hang all the law and the prophets.

While the Pharisees were gathered together, Jesus asked them,

Saying, What think ye of Christ? whose son is he? They say unto him, The son of David.

He saith unto them, How then doth David in spirit call him Lord, saying,

The LORD said unto my Lord, Sit thou on my right hand, till I make thine enemies thy footstool?

If David then call him Lord, how is he his son?

And no man was able to answer him a word, neither durst any man from that day forth ask him any more questions.

Then spake Jesus to the multitude, and to his disciples,

Saying The scribes and the Pharisees sit in Moses' seat:

All therefore whatsoever they bid you observe, that observe and do; but do not ye after their works: for they say, and do not.

For they bind heavy burdens and grievous to be borne, and lay them on men's shoulders; but they themselves will not move them with one of their fingers.

But all their works they do for to be seen of men: they make broad their phylacteries, and enlarge the borders of their garments,

And love the uppermost rooms at feasts, and the chief seats in the synagogues,

And greetings in the markets, and to be called of men, Rabbi, Rabbi.

But be not ye called Rabbi: for one is your Master, even Christ; and all ye are brethren.

And call no man your father upon the earth: for one is your Father, which is in heaven.

Neither be ye called masters: for one is your Master, even Christ.

But he that is greatest among you shall be your servant.

And whosoever shall exalt himself shall be abased; and he that shall humble himself shall be exalted.

But woe unto you, scribes and Pharisees, hypocrites! for ye shut up the kingdom of heaven against men: for ye neither go in yourselves, neither suffer ye them that are entering to go in.

Woe unto you, scribes and Pharisees, hypocrites! for ye devour widows' houses, and for a pretence make long prayer: therefore ye shall receive the greater damnation.

Woe unto you, scribes and Pharisees, hypocrites! for ye compass sea and land to make one proselyte, and when he is made, ye make him twofold more the child of hell than yourselves.

Woe unto you, ye blind guides, which say, Whosoever shall swear by the temple, it is nothing; but whosoever shall swear by the gold of the temple, he is a debtor!

Ye fools and blind: for whether is greater, the gold, or the temple that sanctifieth the gold?

And, Whosoever shall swear by the altar, it is nothing; but whosoever sweareth by the gift that is upon it, he is guilty.

Ye fools and blind: for whether is greater, the gift, or the altar that sanctifieth the gift?

Whoso therefore shall swear by the altar, sweareth by it, and by all things thereon.

And whoso shall swear by the temple, sweareth by it, and by him that dwelleth therein.·

And he that shall swear by heaven, sweareth by the throne of God, and by him that sitteth thereon.

Woe unto you, scribes and Pharisees, hypocrites! for ye pay tithe of mint and anise and cummin, and have omitted the weightier matters of the law, judgment, mercy, and faith: these ought ye to have done, and not to leave the other undone.

Ye blind guides, which strain at a gnat, and swallow a camel.

Woe unto you, scribes and Pharisees, hypocrites! for ye make clean the outside of the cup and of the platter, but within they are full of extortion and excess.

Thou blind Pharisee, cleanse first that which is within the cup and platter, that the outside of them may be clean also.

Woe unto you, scribes and Pharisees, hypocrites! for ye are like unto whited sepulchres, which indeed appear beautiful outward, but are within full of dead men's bones, and of all uncleanness.

Even so ye also outwardly appear righteous unto men, but within ye are full of hypocrisy and iniquity.

Woe unto you, scribes and Pharisees, hypocrites! because ye build the tombs of the prophets, and garnish the sepulchres of the righteous,

And say, If we had been in the days of our fathers, we would not have been partakers with them in the blood of the prophets.

Wherefore ye be witnesses unto yourselves, that ye are the children of them which killed the prophets.

Fill ye up then the measure of your fathers.

Ye serpents, ye generation of vipers, how can ye escape the damnation of hell?

Wherefore, behold, I send unto you prophets, and wise men, and scribes: and some of them ye shall kill and crucify; and some of them shall ye scourge in your synagogues, and persecute them from city to city:

That upon you may come all the righteous blood shed upon the earth, from the blood of righteous Abel unto the blood of Zacharias son of Barachias, whom ye slew between the temple and the altar.

Verily I say unto you, All these things shall come upon this generation.

O Jerusalem, Jerusalem, thou that killest the prophets, and stonest them which are sent unto thee, how often would I have gathered thy children together, even

as a hen gathereth her chickens under her wings, and ye
would not!

Behold, your house is left unto you desolate.

For I say unto you, Ye shall not see me henceforth,
till ye shall say, Blessed is he that cometh in the name of
the Lord. (Matt 21:18, 21:23—23:39)

The tension of the Day of Controversy is palpable in Matthew's
treatment. The rulers and officials of the temple—the priests, the
Pharisees, and the Sadducees—challenge Jesus in fast-paced rep-
artee, but through parries and thrusts, Jesus bests them, seemingly,
at every turn. Still, because Jesus came to die and therefore subtly
orchestrate his grisly demise on Good Friday, Jesus has deftly answered at least one question that deflates the enthusiasm of the
crowds of Palm Sunday.

The Palm Sunday crowds are enthused because they thought
the messiah would come to defeat Rome, and that Jesus was that
messiah. But when Jesus says the Jews should pay tribute to Rome,
to "render unto Caesar what is Caesar's," Jesus's popularity plum-
mets. To these Jews, if Jesus does not come to expel Rome then
Jesus is not the messiah. Thus Jesus, himself, engineers the death
he came to endure. Given this unpopular answer, the crowds will
no longer be an obstacle to Caiaphas's plans. Because of Jesus's intentional answer to this question about taxes, he can hereafter be
crucified with relative impunity. He came to die, and by his care-
fully crafted answer, Jesus both defeats the inquisitor's challenge
and yet paves the way to the very death he came to endure.

Even so, the bottom line is this. On Tuesday of passion week
the rulers of the Jews, the priests, the Pharisees, and the Sadducees, put Jesus on trial, but Jesus turns the tables and judges them
instead. The judges appointed by God to rule God's people find
themselves judged by Jesus, and they earn a failing grade. Jesus
chides them with vitriol unlike any other language attributed to
Jesus in the New Testament:

Woe unto you, scribes and Pharisees, hypocrites! for ye
pay tithe of mint and anise and cummin, and have omitted the weightier matters of the law, judgment, mercy,

and faith: these ought ye to have done, and not to leave the other undone. Ye blind guides, which strain at a gnat, and swallow a camel. Woe unto you, scribes and Pharisees, hypocrites! for ye make clean the outside of the cup and of the platter, but within they are full of extortion and excess. Thou blind Pharisee, cleanse first that which is within the cup and platter, that the outside of them may be clean also. Woe unto you, scribes and Pharisees, hypocrites! for ye are like unto whited sepulchres, which indeed appear beautiful outward, but are within full of dead men's bones, and of all uncleanness. Even so ye also outwardly appear righteous unto men, but within ye are full of hypocrisy and iniquity. . . . Ye serpents, ye generation of vipers, how can ye escape the damnation of hell? (Matt 23:23–28, 33)

Nowhere else in Scripture does Jesus speak so bluntly as he does here on the Tuesday of passion week. Those who came to judge Jesus find themselves judged instead by him, and harshly so. Jesus judges the judges and finds them lacking. God has appointed these priests, these scribes, these Sadducees, and the Pharisees to rule over his people, to judge his people. But those judges have violated their trust. Indeed, rather than serve God consistently with the trust God placed in them, these rulers have turned on God's appointed, God's very Son, the heir to the householder (Matt 21:33–43).

Now we turn to the psalm of the day for Tuesday.

The psalm of the day for Tuesday, selected by the Jewish priests five hundred years before Christ, was Ps 82. That psalm is one often misunderstood and, if not misquoted, certainly cited for erroneous conclusions. Here is what it says:

God standeth in the congregation of the mighty; he judgeth among the gods.

How long will ye judge unjustly, and accept the persons of the wicked? Selah.

Defend the poor and fatherless: do justice to the afflicted and needy.

Deliver the poor and needy: rid them out of the hand of the wicked.

They know not, neither will they understand; they walk on in darkness: all the foundations of the earth are out of course.

I have said, Ye are gods; and all of you are children of the most High.

But ye shall die like men, and fall like one of the princes.

Arise, O God, judge the earth: for thou shalt inherit all nations.

John Phillips says Ps 82 "is concerned with a universal problem[,] . . . the problem of the unjust judge. . . . The judges suddenly find themselves in court . . . [and] not arrogantly sitting on the bench. . . . They are in the dock, and God sits upon the bench."[1] God is judging the judges.

Verse one of Ps 82 uses language that startles the monotheist, saying, "God standeth in the congregation of the mighty; he judgeth among the gods." Despite this unsettling verbiage, Ps 82 does not endorse polytheism. Phillips explains:

> The word *elohim* occurs twice in this verse but with differing values. The first time the Holy Spirit uses an intensive plural, and it is the name for God the Creator. The second use of the word is called a simple plural; it is used to describe those who make up the assembly of God—the judges of God's people Israel. They are called *elohim* because they are His delegates—their authority derives from Him. . . . [They are] appointed to represent His throne, to administer His will. . . .
>
> He [the Lord] has suddenly come into His court and the judges now find themselves the judged.[2]

As Phillips explains, the key to understanding Ps 82 lies with identifying God and "the gods." God's identity is self-evident; he is the great I AM. The lower case "gods," however, are not deities. The "gods" are, instead, the "judges of God's people Israel."[3]

---

1. Phillips, *Exploring the Psalms*, 1:674.
2. Phillips, *Exploring the Psalms*, 1:675.
3. Phillips, *Exploring the Psalms*, 1:675.

With the actors identified, God and the judges he has appointed to govern Israel, the meaning of Ps 82 becomes clear. God not only judges his judges, but God finds them guilty. They have not judged fairly; they have not kept the faith. God's appointed rulers, these "gods," have favored the rich and powerful, and shown partiality to the wicked. God's judges have failed. That is the thrust of Ps 82.

This interpretation of Ps 82 suggests the psalm's correlation to Tuesday of passion week. In Ps 82, the psalm of Tuesday, God judges and fails his judges. On Tuesday of passion week, God again judges his judges, the Sanhedrin, the priests, the scribes, and their attempt to judge and condemn Jesus. By their inquisitions, God's appointed rulers of his people Israel intend to unmask Jesus as a pretender and charlatan. But Jesus, instead, judges them. And they fail—miserably. It is so blatant a failure that Jesus levels at them a disgust that rings out from the pages of the Gospels. You hypocrites! Jesus exclaims.

Not only have the priests and their allies failed, but those unjust judges in their failure have shaken the very "foundations of the earth," the same Earth that God created on the third day (Tuesday) of creation week (cf. Ps 82:5 and Gen 1:9–10).

To summarize, then:

1. On Tuesday of creation week, God created the earth.

2. In the psalm of the day for Tuesday, Ps 82, God judges the very judges whom he has selected to rule his people, judges whose corrupt judgments have shaken the very foundations of the Earth that God created and which he owns by right of creation.

3. On Tuesday of passion week, those very judges selected by God seek to judge and condemn Jesus, but Jesus instead judges them and finds them woefully inadequate, declaring of them, "Ye serpents, ye generation of vipers, how can ye escape the damnation of hell?" (Matt 23:33)

Through day three, then, the record remains unbroken. Parallels exist between the weeks in Scripture, including obvious interface between the psalm of the day for Tuesday, Ps 82, selected by the priests about 500 BC, and the events of Tuesday in passion week, five hundred years later. We are three for three and proving "daily" that only God, not those postexilic priests, could have known what would happen to Jesus on Tuesday of passion week, five hundred years after Ps 82 was selected.

6.

The Fourth Day (Wednesday)

ON WEDNESDAY, THE FOURTH day of creation week, Gen 1 tells us:

> And God said, Let there be lights in the firmament of the heaven to divide the day from the night; and let them be for signs, and for seasons, and for days, and years: and let them be for lights in the firmament of the heaven to give light upon the earth: and it was so. And God made two great lights; the greater light to rule the day, and the lesser light to rule the night: *he made* the stars also. And God set them in the firmament of the heaven to give light upon the earth, and to rule over the day and over the night, and to divide the light from the darkness: and God saw that *it was* good. And the evening and the morning were the fourth day. (vv. 14–19)

On the first day of creation, God had created light and dark, day and night. On Wednesday, the fourth day, Gen 1 says he created a great light (the sun) to rule the day and a lesser light (the moon) to rule the night, to separate light from darkness. As on the first day, we are reminded of how John treats light and dark throughout his Gospel and even calls Jesus the Light. John the apostle says his namesake, John the Baptizer, was sent "to bear witness of the Light. . . . He [the Baptizer] was not that Light, but was sent to bear witness of that Light. That was the true Light, which lighteth every man that cometh into the world" (John 1:7–9).

The events of Wednesday of passion week, as found in the Gospel of Mark, are as follows:

> After two days was the feast of the passover, and of unleavened bread: and the chief priests and the scribes sought how they might take him by craft, and put him to death. But they said, Not on the feast day, lest there be an uproar of the people. And being in Bethany in the house of Simon the leper, as he sat at meat, there came a woman having an alabaster box of ointment of spikenard very precious; and she brake the box, and poured it on his head. And there were some that had indignation within themselves, and said, Why was this waste of the ointment made? For it might have been sold for more than three hundred pence, and have been given to the poor. And they murmured against her. And Jesus said, Let her alone; why trouble ye her? she hath wrought a good work on me. For ye have the poor with you always, and whensoever ye will ye may do them good: but me ye have not always. She hath done what she could: she is come aforehand to anoint my body to the burying. Verily I say unto you, Wheresoever this gospel shall be preached throughout the whole world, this also that she hath done shall be spoken of for a memorial of her. And Judas Iscariot, one of the twelve, went unto the chief priests, to betray him unto them. And when they heard it, they were glad, and promised to give him money. And he sought how he might conveniently betray him.
> (Mark 14:1–11)

Wednesday of passion week is sometimes called the Day of Rest because we know so little about what Jesus did that day. And certainly, after the anxious, frenetic events of Tuesday, the Day of Controversy, a restful day was needed. Even so, no amount of rest could prepare Jesus for the events of the coming Thursday and Friday, when the fate of both mankind and God's good creation would be determined under the highest stakes and the greatest pressure imaginable.

Rest is exactly what Jesus needed.

Even so, though Jesus rested, our knowledge of passion week's Wednesday is not a nullity. Mark's Gospel tells us much of what occurred on Passion Wednesday. First, the Jewish leaders, the chief priests and scribes, plotted the best way to kill Jesus, though mindful that they needed yet to erode Jesus's popularity with the masses. Matthew tells us Caiaphas leads the conspiracy (Matt 26:3–5). Second, Jesus and at least some of the disciples ate dinner Wednesday night in Bethany at the home of Simon, called the leper. At that meal, a woman (John seems to identify her as Mary, sister of risen Lazarus) pours a costly elixir on Jesus's head, seemingly a pre-death anointing of Jesus for burial. And at least one disciple (Judas Iscariot) objects. Third, Jesus corrects the objector, telling him that Mary's deed will be remembered wherever the gospel of salvation is preached. And Jesus speaks of his impending burial, suggesting that Jesus knows of the evil plans to kill him. Fourth, ominously, Judas retires to the priests and offers to betray Jesus for money (Mark 14:1–11).

The other Gospels add still other details to the Wednesday events. Luke tells us that Satan actually entered into Judas, inducing Judas to betray Jesus evilly (Luke 22:1–6). Matthew tells us that Jesus knew of Judas's impending betrayal and of the cruel death he was to suffer. Jesus actually warns the disciples he would soon be both betrayed and crucified (Matt 26:1–16).

Nevertheless, the fact that Jesus's activities on Wednesday of passion week were so limited, or at least under reported, caused me to worry that it might be impossible to match up the events of Passion Wednesday and the Wednesday psalm of the day. I was wrong.

Two things are clear from the Gospels: First, evil is afoot. Caiaphas and his ilk plot the crucifixion of Jesus. Judas objects to Mary's act of love toward Jesus, and Satan enters into Judas, leading Judas to betray Jesus. Second, Jesus knows of this evil; he knows what is happening. He warns the disciples that he will soon be betrayed and crucified. Jesus knows the evil.

In sum, evil looms, seemingly secretly, but Jesus nevertheless knows.

The psalm of the day for Wednesday is Ps 94:

> O Lord God, to whom vengeance belongeth; O God, to whom vengeance belongeth, shew thyself.
>
> Lift up thyself, thou judge of the earth: render a reward to the proud.
>
> LORD, how long shall the wicked, how long shall the wicked triumph?
>
> How long shall they utter and speak hard things? and all the workers of iniquity boast themselves?
>
> They break in pieces thy people, O LORD, and afflict thine heritage.
>
> They slay the widow and the stranger, and murder the fatherless.
>
> Yet they say, The LORD shall not see, neither shall the God of Jacob regard it.
>
> Understand, ye brutish among the people: and ye fools, when will ye be wise?
>
> He that planted the ear, shall he not hear? he that formed the eye, shall he not see?
>
> He that chastiseth the heathen, shall not he correct? he that teacheth man knowledge, shall not he know?
>
> The LORD knoweth the thoughts of man, that they are vanity.
>
> Blessed is the man whom thou chastenest, O LORD, and teachest him out of thy law;
>
> That thou mayest give him rest from the days of adversity, until the pit be digged for the wicked.
>
> For the LORD will not cast off his people, neither will he forsake his inheritance.
>
> But judgment shall return unto righteousness: and all the upright in heart shall follow it.
>
> Who will rise up for me against the evildoers? or who will stand up for me against the workers of iniquity?
>
> Unless the LORD had been my help, my soul had almost dwelt in silence.
>
> When I said, My foot slippeth; thy mercy, O LORD, held me up.

> In the multitude of my thoughts within me thy comforts delight my soul.
>
> Shall the throne of iniquity have fellowship with thee, which frameth mischief by a law?
>
> They gather themselves together against the soul of the righteous, and condemn the innocent blood.
>
> But the LORD is my defence; and my God is the rock of my refuge.
>
> And he shall bring upon them their own iniquity, and shall cut them off in their own wickedness; yea, the LORD our God shall cut them off.

The psalm's origins are unclear. John Phillips says neither its author nor its date of origin can be firmly established.[1] Even so, Ps 94 appears to originate from the early postexilic era, when the faithful remnant struggled to rebuild Jerusalem's walls and the temple, while enduring opposition from multiple quarters. God willed the remnant to complete the rebuilds, but evil opposed them (see Ezra 4–5; Neh 4, 6).

The era of origin may be another time, but the context of Ps 94 fits the postexilic era nevertheless. God's faithful remnant works diligently to perform God's will, to rebuild both the temple and the walls of Jerusalem. But evil abounds, attempting to sabotage God's will by subterfuge, betrayal, and deceit. And the psalmist, whomever he was, bemoans the conflict:

> O God, to whom vengeance belongeth, shew thyself.
>
> Lift up thyself, thou judge of the earth: render a reward to the proud.
>
> LORD, how long shall the wicked, how long shall the wicked triumph?
>
> How long shall they utter and speak hard things? and all the workers of iniquity boast themselves?
>
> They break in pieces thy people, O LORD, and afflict thine heritage.
>
> They slay the widow and the stranger, and murder the fatherless. (Ps 94:1–6)

---

1. Phillips, *Exploring the Psalms*, 2:53.

Similarly, on Wednesday of passion week, as Jesus presumably rests from the confrontational chaos of Tuesday, the Day of Controversy, evil quietly but effectively works to alienate Judas, trigger the betrayal of the Christ, and pay the betrayer his thirty pieces of silver. Evil makes its moves.

In each case, whether post exile or during passion week, evil believes it operates unbeknownst to God, in private, undetected. But God knows. In the context of Ps 94:

> Yet they say, The LORD shall not see, neither shall the God of Jacob regard it.
>
> Understand, ye brutish among the people: and ye fools, when will ye be wise?
>
> He that planted the ear, shall he not hear? he that formed the eye, shall he not see?
>
> He that chastiseth the heathen, shall not he correct? he that teacheth man knowledge, shall not he know?
>
> The LORD knoweth the thoughts of man, that they are vanity. (Ps 94:7–11)

Wednesday of passion week proceeds similarly. The Jewish leaders, the chief priests and scribes, plot how to kill Jesus, mindful that they need first to erode Jesus's popularity with the masses. Chief priest Caiaphas leads the conspiracy. Jesus eats dinner in Bethany at the home of Simon, the leper. At that meal, Mary, sister of the risen Lazarus, pours a costly oil on Jesus's head, a pre-death anointing of Jesus for burial. Judas objects and earns Jesus's reprimand. Satan, himself, enters Judas and causes Judas to sneak to the priests to bargain to betray Jesus.

Evil abounds on Wednesday of passion week, acting, it thinks, in secret, just as it did in the context of Wednesday's psalm, Ps 94.

But God knows. God knew the evil that opposed the rebuilding of Jerusalem and the temple (Ps 94). And God, the Son, knew the evil that swirled about him on Wednesday of passion week. Jesus told the disciples he was to be crucified and die. He knew the machinations of Judas and the plots of Caiaphas. Jesus knew of Judas's impending betrayal and of the barbaric death he was to suffer, actually warning the disciples he would soon be both betrayed and crucified (Matt 26:1–16).

God knew. Just as Ps 94 foresees it, evil abounds, but God knows. Wednesday of passion week, then, mirrors the theme of the Wednesday psalm, Ps 94. Evil abounds, it thinks, in secret. But God knows.

To summarize, then:

1. On Wednesday of creation week, God created the lights that govern day and night, light and dark, and, symbolically, good and evil.

2. In the psalm of the day for Wednesday, Ps 94, evil abounds in supposed secret, attempting to foil God's will, the rebuilding of Jerusalem and the temple, but the secrecy craved by evil does not exist because God knows the evil thoughts, plans, and actions of devious mankind.

3. On Wednesday of passion week, evil men move to eliminate Jesus, thinking their dastardly deeds and intentions are secret, but Jesus knows what they are doing and warns of the terror to follow.

Evil proliferates, seemingly in secret, but God knows. The parallels are clear.

Through day four, Wednesday, the record remains unbroken. We are four for four. Symmetries exist between the weeks in Scripture, including obvious interface between the psalm of the day for Wednesday, Ps 94, selected by the priests in 500 BC, and the events of Wednesday in passion week, at least five hundred years later. Only God, not those priests, could have known what would happen to Jesus on Wednesday of passion week.

Conclusion: One singular intelligence selected the psalms of the day to correspond to the events of passion week five hundred years later. And that singular intelligence can only be the great I AM, the God of Heaven. No one else.

The proof piles up.

7.

The Fifth Day (Thursday)

On Thursday, Day Five of creation week, Gen 1 says this:

> And God said, Let the waters bring forth abundantly
> the moving creature that hath life, and fowl that may fly
> above the earth in the open firmament of heaven. And
> God created great whales, and every living creature that
> moveth, which the waters brought forth abundantly, af-
> ter their kind, and every winged fowl after his kind: and
> God saw that it was good. And God blessed them, saying,
> Be fruitful, and multiply, and fill the waters in the seas,
> and let fowl multiply in the earth. And the evening and
> the morning were the fifth day. (vv. 20–23)

On Thursday of creation week, then, God created aquatic creatures
and birds of the air. Each of those ultimately, but not immediately,
become staples in mankind's diet (see Gen 9:1–3).

On Thursday of passion week, day five, Mark tells us this:

> And the first day of unleavened bread, when they killed
> the passover, his disciples said unto him, Where wilt thou
> that we go and prepare that thou mayest eat the passover?

And he sendeth forth two of his disciples, and saith unto them, Go ye into the city, and there shall meet you a man bearing a pitcher of water: follow him.

And wheresoever he shall go in, say ye to the goodman of the house, The Master saith, Where is the guestchamber, where I shall eat the passover with my disciples?

And he will shew you a large upper room furnished and prepared: there make ready for us.

And his disciples went forth, and came into the city, and found as he had said unto them: and they made ready the passover.

And in the evening he cometh with the twelve.

And as they sat and did eat, Jesus said, Verily I say unto you, One of you which eateth with me shall betray me.

And they began to be sorrowful, and to say unto him one by one, Is it I? and another said, Is it I?

And he answered and said unto them, It is one of the twelve, that dippeth with me in the dish.

The Son of man indeed goeth, as it is written of him: but woe to that man by whom the Son of man is betrayed! good were it for that man if he had never been born.

And as they did eat, Jesus took bread, and blessed, and brake it, and gave to them, and said, Take, eat: this is my body.

And he took the cup, and when he had given thanks, he gave it to them: and they all drank of it.

And he said unto them, This is my blood of the new testament, which is shed for many.

Verily I say unto you, I will drink no more of the fruit of the vine, until that day that I drink it new in the kingdom of God.

And when they had sung an hymn, they went out into the mount of Olives.

And Jesus saith unto them, All ye shall be offended because of me this night: for it is written, I will smite the shepherd, and the sheep shall be scattered.

But after that I am risen, I will go before you into Galilee.

But Peter said unto him, Although all shall be offended, yet will not I.

And Jesus saith unto him, Verily I say unto thee, That this day, even in this night, before the cock crow twice, thou shalt deny me thrice.

But he spake the more vehemently, If I should die with thee, I will not deny thee in any wise. Likewise also said they all.

And they came to a place which was named Gethsemane: and he saith to his disciples, Sit ye here, while I shall pray.

And he taketh with him Peter and James and John, and began to be sore amazed, and to be very heavy;

And saith unto them, My soul is exceeding sorrowful unto death: tarry ye here, and watch.

And he went forward a little, and fell on the ground, and prayed that, if it were possible, the hour might pass from him.

And he said, Abba, Father, all things are possible unto thee; take away this cup from me: nevertheless not what I will, but what thou wilt.

And he cometh, and findeth them sleeping, and saith unto Peter, Simon, sleepest thou? couldest not thou watch one hour?

Watch ye and pray, lest ye enter into temptation. The spirit truly is ready, but the flesh is weak.

And again he went away, and prayed, and spake the same words.

And when he returned, he found them asleep again, (for their eyes were heavy,) neither wist they what to answer him.

And he cometh the third time, and saith unto them, Sleep on now, and take your rest: it is enough, the hour is come; behold, the Son of man is betrayed into the hands of sinners.

Rise up, let us go; lo, he that betrayeth me is at hand.

And immediately, while he yet spake, cometh Judas, one of the twelve, and with him a great multitude with swords and staves, from the chief priests and the scribes and the elders.

> And he that betrayed him had given them a token, saying, Whomsoever I shall kiss, that same is he; take him, and lead him away safely.
>
> And as soon as he was come, he goeth straightway to him, and saith, Master, master; and kissed him.
>
> And they laid their hands on him, and took him.
>
> And one of them that stood by drew a sword, and smote a servant of the high priest, and cut off his ear.
>
> And Jesus answered and said unto them, Are ye come out, as against a thief, with swords and with staves to take me?
>
> I was daily with you in the temple teaching, and ye took me not: but the scriptures must be fulfilled.
>
> And they all forsook him, and fled.
>
> And there followed him a certain young man, having a linen cloth cast about his naked body; and the young men laid hold on him:
>
> And he left the linen cloth, and fled from them naked. (Mark 14:12–52)

Clearly, passion week's Thursday is a busy and important day, the most telling and long-lasting event being Jesus's celebrating the Passover Feast while instituting a new celebratory feast for Christians, the Lord's Supper. Indeed, the juxtaposition of the two memorials, Passover and the Lord's Supper, would seem to connect the two indelibly and make abundantly clear that Passover, by which God's people were redeemed from Egyptian slavery, and Easter, by which all God's people are redeemed from sin's slavery, are prophetic mirror images of one another. Passover is the great dress rehearsal for the even greater Easter.

There is more to passion week's Thursday though. As Mark portrays the day, the following occurred:

1. Jesus prepared to eat, and did eat, the Passover meal (vv. 12–17).

2. Jesus did institute still another feast or meal, what many Christians today call the Lord's Supper (vv. 22–25).

3. While eating the Passover, Jesus announces to the Twelve that one of them will betray him (vv. 18–21) and Matt 26 identifies Judas Iscariot.

4. Jesus informs the disciples that they will that evening "be scattered" and that Peter will deny him three times (vv. 27–31).

5. Having finished the Passover Feast, Jesus and the disciples, less Judas, relocate to Gethsemane, where Jesus, in the company of Peter, James, and John, prays the most heartbreaking of prayers (vv. 35–39).

6. Jesus is betrayed by Judas into the hands of the Temple guards, whose intent is to carry out the death of Jesus as planned by the temple hierarchy (vv. 43–50).

Against this backdrop, we turn to the psalm of the day for Thursday. That psalm, selected five hundred years before Christ, is Ps 81, which reads,

> Sing aloud unto God our strength: make a joyful noise unto the God of Jacob.
> Take a psalm, and bring hither the timbrel, the pleasant harp with the psaltery.
> Blow up the trumpet in the new moon, in the time appointed, on our solemn feast day.
> For this was a statute for Israel, and a law of the God of Jacob.
> This he ordained in Joseph for a testimony, when he went out through the land of Egypt: where I heard a language that I understood not.
> I removed his shoulder from the burden: his hands were delivered from the pots.
> Thou calledst in trouble, and I delivered thee; I answered thee in the secret place of thunder: I proved thee at the waters of Meribah. Selah.
> Hear, O my people, and I will testify unto thee: O Israel, if thou wilt hearken unto me;
> There shall no strange god be in thee; neither shalt thou worship any strange god.

> I am the LORD thy God, which brought thee out of the land of Egypt: open thy mouth wide, and I will fill it.
>
> But my people would not hearken to my voice; and Israel would none of me.
>
> So I gave them up unto their own hearts' lust: and they walked in their own counsels.
>
> Oh that my people had hearkened unto me, and Israel had walked in my ways!
>
> I should soon have subdued their enemies, and turned my hand against their adversaries.
>
> The haters of the LORD should have submitted themselves unto him: but their time should have endured for ever.
>
> He should have fed them also with the finest of the wheat: and with honey out of the rock should I have satisfied thee.

Psalm 81 celebrates the great feast commemorating God's great deeds. (Blow up the trumpet in the new moon, in the time appointed, on our solemn feast day. Verse 3.) Verses 1 through 5 reference the feast, which God decreed to memorialize his redemption of his people from their enslavement to the most powerful nation on earth at the time, Egypt, the great cradle of civilization. This marvelous and unprecedented deed of God's munificent power freed the pharaoh's massive labor force from Egypt's dominion without one slave raising a hand to oppose Egypt. God alone did it. These are those verses:

> Sing aloud unto God our strength: make a joyful noise unto the God of Jacob.
>
> Take a psalm, and bring hither the timbrel, the pleasant harp with the psaltery.
>
> Blow up the trumpet in the new moon, in the time appointed, on our solemn feast day.
>
> For this was a statute for Israel, and a law of the God of Jacob.
>
> This he ordained in Joseph for a testimony, when he went out through the land of Egypt: where I heard a language that I understood not. (vv. 1–5)

And the feast that Jesus ordained on Thursday of passion week, the Lord's Supper, regales an even more astonishing accomplishment of God—that is, the redemption of all mankind from slavery to sin, to the "god" of this world, to Satan, a being infinitely more powerful even than Egypt's pharaoh. This redemption also occurs without input, without aggressive act, from any of sin's slaves. The wondrous result occurs via God's power alone. And God bestows it upon us through his grace. It is God's gift to us, just as was Israel's freedom from Egypt.

Once again, the parallels are clear. The psalm selected for Thursday worship in the temple circa 500 BC, and used thereafter for Thursday worship so long as the temple remained, anticipates and celebrates the emancipation from Egypt by way of the Passover Feast. Similarly, on Thursday of passion week, Jesus and his disciples partake of the Passover Feast and institute another, the Lord's Supper, which celebrates a greater emancipation. There are, then, clear, undeniable connections between the psalm of the day and the events of passion week's Thursday, five hundred years later. The priests in 500 BC could not have known or anticipated this.

But God did.

And that means that the intelligence that selected Ps 81 for Thursday's worship is an intelligence that spanned those five hundred years and knew in advance its plans for passion week in the distant future.

That intelligence was the Redeemer God, the great I AM.

It could be no other.

8.

The Sixth Day (Friday)

ON FRIDAY, THE SIXTH day of creation week, Gen 1 says this occurred:

> And God said, Let the earth bring forth the living crea-
> ture after his kind, cattle, and creeping thing, and beast
> of the earth after his kind: and it was so. And God made
> the beast of the earth after his kind, and cattle after their
> kind, and every thing that creepeth upon the earth af-
> ter his kind: and God saw that it was good. And God
> said, Let us make man in our image, after our likeness:
> and let them have dominion over the fish of the sea, and
> over the fowl of the air, and over the cattle, and over all
> the earth, and over every creeping thing that creepeth
> upon the earth. So God created man in his own image,
> in the image of God created he him; male and female
> created he them. And God blessed them, and God said
> unto them, Be fruitful, and multiply, and replenish the
> earth, and subdue it: and have dominion over the fish
> of the sea, and over the fowl of the air, and over every
> living thing that moveth upon the earth. And God said,
> Behold, I have given you every herb bearing seed, which
> is upon the face of all the earth, and every tree, in the
> which is the fruit of a tree yielding seed; to you it shall
> be for meat. And to every beast of the earth, and to every
> fowl of the air, and to every thing that creepeth upon

> the earth, wherein there is life, I have given every green
> herb for meat: and it was so. And God saw every thing
> that he had made, and, behold, it was very good. And the
> evening and the morning were the sixth day. (vv. 24–29)

On this sixth day of creation, per Gen 1, God created land creatures and, especially, mankind, and he charged mankind with the
responsibility to rule, to "have dominion . . . over every living thing
that moveth upon the earth" (v. 28). Randy Alcorn says this verse
establishes that man, before the fall, was called to reign as king(s)
of God's creation.[1] Alcorn points out that this pronouncement of
man's role in God's plan from the Bible's first chapter is reiterated
in its last where God announces that his servants will "reign for-
ever and ever" on the new Earth (Rev 22:5). In a real sense, God's
initial plan for mankind was to reign as kings of the Earth.

Nevertheless, due to man's fall, and the consequent curse of
sin, man could no longer fulfill the role of God's ruler, and it became Christ's place to serve and rule.

The events of Friday of passion week are, of course, infamous.
Good Friday is the day of Jesus's crucifixion, at once the darkest
and brightest of all days. The details are numerous, but the following verses from Mark 15 focus on Jesus's appearance before
Pilate and his crucifixion thereafter. Readers can neither miss nor
overlook the peculiar emphasis upon Jesus as King:

> And straightway in the morning the chief priests held a
> consultation with the elders and scribes and the whole
> council, and bound Jesus, and carried him away, and
> delivered him to Pilate.
>
> And *Pilate asked him, Art thou the King of the Jews?*
> *And he answering said unto them, Thou sayest it.*
>
> And the chief priests accused him of many things:
> but he answered nothing.
>
> And Pilate asked him again, saying, Answerest thou
> nothing? behold how many things they witness against
> thee.

---

1. Alcorn, *Heaven*, 217.

But Jesus yet answered nothing; so that Pilate marvelled.

Now at that feast he released unto them one prisoner, whomsoever they desired.

And there was one named Barabbas, which lay bound with them that had made insurrection with him, who had committed murder in the insurrection.

And the multitude crying aloud began to desire him to do as he had ever done unto them.

But *Pilate answered them, saying, Will ye that I release unto you the King of the Jews?*

For he knew that the chief priests had delivered him for envy.

But the chief priests moved the people, that he should rather release Barabbas unto them.

And Pilate answered and said again unto them, *What will ye then that I shall do unto him whom ye call the King of the Jews?*

And they cried out again, Crucify him.

Then Pilate said unto them, Why, what evil hath he done? And they cried out the more exceedingly, Crucify him.

And so Pilate, willing to content the people, released Barabbas unto them, and delivered Jesus, when he had scourged him, to be crucified.

And the soldiers led him away into the hall, called Praetorium; and they call together the whole band.

And *they clothed him with purple, and platted a crown of thorns,* and put it about his head,

And began to salute him, *Hail, King of the Jews!*

And they smote him on the head with a reed, and did spit upon him, and bowing their knees worshipped him.

And when they had mocked him, they took off the purple from him, and put his own clothes on him, and led him out to crucify him.

And they compel one Simon a Cyrenian, who passed by, coming out of the country, the father of Alexander and Rufus, to bear his cross.

And they bring him unto the place Golgotha, which is, being interpreted, The place of a skull.

And they gave him to drink wine mingled with myrrh: but he received it not.

And when they had crucified him, they parted his garments, casting lots upon them, what every man should take.

And it was the third hour, and they crucified him.

And the superscription of his accusation was written over, THE KING OF THE JEWS.

And with him they crucify two thieves; the one on his right hand, and the other on his left.

And the scripture was fulfilled, which saith, And he was numbered with the transgressors.

And they that passed by railed on him, wagging their heads, and saying, Ah, thou that destroyest the temple, and buildest it in three days,

Save thyself, and come down from the cross.

Likewise also *the chief priests mocking said* among themselves with the scribes, He saved others; himself he cannot save.

Let Christ the King of Israel descend now from the cross, that we may see and believe. And they that were crucified with him reviled him.

And when the sixth hour was come, there was darkness over the whole land until the ninth hour.

And at the ninth hour Jesus cried with a loud voice, saying, Eloi, Eloi, lama sabachthani? which is, being interpreted, My God, my God, why hast thou forsaken me?

And some of them that stood by, when they heard it, said, Behold, he calleth Elias.

And one ran and filled a sponge full of vinegar, and put it on a reed, and gave him to drink, saying, Let alone; let us see whether Elias will come to take him down.

And Jesus cried with a loud voice, and gave up the ghost.

And the veil of the temple was rent in twain from the top to the bottom. (Mark 15:1–38, emphasis added)

Seldom does the New Testament focus on the kingship of Jesus with the laser like clarity that we see here:

- "Pilate asked him, Art thou the King of the Jews?" (v. 2)

- "Pilate answered them, saying, Will ye that I release unto you the King of the Jews?" (v. 9).

- "Pilate answered and said again unto them, What will ye then that I shall do unto him whom ye call the King of the Jews?" (v. 12).

- "And they clothed him with purple, and platted a crown of thorns, and put it about his head, And began to salute him, Hail, King of the Jews!" (vv. 17–18).

- "And the superscription of his accusation was written over, THE KING OF THE JEWS" (v. 26).

- "Let Christ the King of Israel descend now from the cross, that we may see and believe. And they that were crucified with him reviled him" (v. 32).

But we are not finished. John's Gospel adds even more detail.

> Then Pilate entered into the judgment hall again, and called Jesus, and said unto him, *Art thou the King of the Jews?*
>
> Jesus answered him, Sayest thou this thing of thyself, or did others tell it thee of me?
>
> Pilate answered, Am I a Jew? Thine own nation and the chief priests have delivered thee unto me: what hast thou done?
>
> Jesus answered, *My kingdom is not of this world: if my kingdom were of this world, then would my servants fight, that I should not be delivered to the Jews: but now is my kingdom not from hence.*
>
> Pilate therefore said unto him, *Art thou a king then?* Jesus answered, *Thou sayest that I am a king. To this end was I born, and for this cause came I into the world,* that I should bear witness unto the truth. Every one that is of the truth heareth my voice.
>
> Pilate saith unto him, What is truth? And when he had said this, he went out again unto the Jews, and saith unto them, I find in him no fault at all.

But ye have a custom, that I should release unto you one at the passover: *will ye therefore that I release unto you the King of the Jews?* . . .

Then Pilate therefore took Jesus, and scourged him.

And the *soldiers platted a crown of thorns, and put it on his head,* and they *put on him a purple robe,*

And said, *Hail, King of the Jews!* . . .

And from thenceforth Pilate sought to release him: but the Jews cried out, saying, If thou let this man go, thou art not Caesar's friend: *whosoever maketh himself a king speaketh against Caesar.*

When Pilate therefore heard that saying, he brought Jesus forth, and sat down in the judgment seat in a place that is called the Pavement, but in the Hebrew, Gabbatha.

And it was the preparation of the passover, and about the sixth hour: *and he saith unto the Jews, Behold your King!*

But they cried out, Away with him, away with him, crucify him. *Pilate saith unto them, Shall I crucify your King? The chief priests answered, We have no king but Caesar.* . . .

Where they crucified him, and two other with him, on either side one, and Jesus in the midst.

And *Pilate wrote a title, and put it on the cross. And the writing was JESUS OF NAZARETH THE KING OF THE JEWS.*

This title then read many of the Jews: for the place where Jesus was crucified was nigh to the city: and *it was written in Hebrew, and Greek, and Latin.*

Then said the chief priests of the Jews to Pilate, Write not, The King of the Jews; but that he said, I am King of the Jews.

Pilate answered, What I have written I have written.
(John 18:33–39; 19:1–3, 12–15, 18–22, emphasis added)

It is no stretch to offer that nowhere in the Gospels is the kingship of Jesus so discussed, debated and addressed as here on Good Friday, the sixth day of passion week. And that fact is the paradigmatic segue into the psalm of the day for Friday, Ps 93, the very theme of which is that the Lord God is King. Here is the text of Ps 93, selected for Friday worship in the temple five hundred years before Jesus's birth:

> The LORD reigneth, he is clothed with majesty; the LORD is clothed with strength, wherewith he hath girded himself: the world also is stablished, that it cannot be moved.
>
> Thy throne is established of old: thou art from everlasting.
>
> The floods have lifted up, O LORD, the floods have lifted up their voice; the floods lift up their waves.
>
> The LORD on high is mightier than the noise of many waters, yea, than the mighty waves of the sea.
>
> Thy testimonies are very sure: holiness becometh thine house, O LORD, for ever.

The psalm, selected so long before, fits exactly the peculiar motif of the trial before Pilate and the crucifixion of Jesus, the King of the Jews. "The LORD reigneth . . . clothed with majesty. . . . [his] throne is established of old . . . from everlasting" (Ps 93:1–2).

He, Jesus, is King!

The pattern of Good Friday, the discussion between Jesus and Pilate, the remonstrations of the Jewish leaders, the rude treatment by the Roman guards, they all bear upon the question whether Jesus is King, a question Jesus answers in the affirmative. And in Ps 93, the psalm selected to govern temple worship on Fridays, beginning five hundred years before Christ, the reign of King Jehovah is celebrated. God's reign as King is the theme. No priest who suggested Ps 93 as the psalm of the day for Fridays could possibly have known what was to happen on the pivotal day of human history, Earth's history: Good Friday in Jerusalem, five hundred years later.

Only God could.

But that is neither the end of the events of Good Friday nor the content of Ps 93.

The debate over Jesus as king is the focus of this discussion to this point, but the greater occurrence of Good Friday, what we best remember it for, is the crucifixion, the cruel execution that

Jesus suffered that day. And Ps 93, with a bit of help from David, addresses that barbarism too.

Verses 3 and 4 of the Friday psalm say this, and its pertinence to the crucifixion of Jesus is provided by David in another psalm of another day:

> The floods have lifted up, O Lord, the floods have lifted up their voice; the floods lift up their waves.
> The Lord on high is mightier than the noise of many waters, yea, than the mighty waves of the sea. (Ps 93:3–4)

These verses emphasize waters, floods that seem to oppose the Lord, the King, whose powers exceed the force of the waters. Verse 3 uses the term "floods" three times in its short nineteen words. And verse 4 references the "many waters" and "mighty waves of the sea" and denotes that the King, "The Lord on high" is mightier than these powerful "waves" or waters. "The Lord on high" prevails over the waters.

Approximately one thousand years before Christ, David wrote two psalms that anticipate the grisly crucifixion of his greater Son, Jesus. These prophetic, crucifixion psalms, Pss 22 and 69, precede by five hundred years or so even the selection of the psalms of the day. Psalm 22 miraculously anticipates the physical torture of crucifixion, the barbaric death of Jesus and the many others who died on the cruel cross. Psalm 22 has obvious connections to Calvary, despite its ancient origins, even beginning with a preview of the most haunting verse in Scripture, "My God, My God, why hast thou forsaken me?" (v. 1).

But Ps 22 is not the one that connects with Ps 93, the Friday psalm. Instead, Ps 69 is that one. While Ps 22 prophetically describes the excruciating physical death suffered by Jesus and others who died on the cruel tree, Ps 69 prophetically describes, instead, the spiritual torture and death which Jesus only and singularly suffered on Calvary. Psalm 69 describes a Savior inundated and overcome by sin to the point where, ultimately, "He who knew no sin became sin for our sakes" (2 Cor 5:21). So desperate was the spiritual anguish endured by Jesus in this unprecedented state, where God the Son was truly forsaken by God the Father, that Jesus wailed out those opening words of Ps 22, "My God, My God, why hast thou forsaken me?"

And importantly for the sake of our discussion here, the figure of speech adopted by David in Ps 69, in approximately 1000 BC, to describe prophetically the inundation of sin over the desperate Savior precisely corresponds to the forces of flooding water, the many waters, the mighty waves of the sea (Ps 93:3–4). These verses from Ps 69 bear this out:

> Save me, O God; for the waters are come in unto my soul.
> I sink in deep mire, where there is no standing: I am come into deep waters, where the floods overflow me.…
> Deliver me out of the mire, and let me not sink: let me be delivered from them that hate me, and out of the deep waters.
> Let not the waterflood overflow me, neither let the deep swallow me up, and let not the pit shut her mouth upon me. (vv. 1–2, 14–15).

When the Friday psalm, Ps 93, is read in conjunction with David's psalm, Ps 69, in which David describes the spiritual death of Jesus though it would not occur until one thousand years later, it is clear that Ps 93 does more than anticipate the debate of Christ's kingship between Pilate, the Roman soldiers, the Jewish hierarchy, and Jesus himself. Psalm 93 also anticipates, as only God himself could, the crucifixion itself, as the King submits willingly to immersion in the mirey waters, the sewerage, of evil sin. And that willing self-emasculation of the Christ is the defining moment of history in which the Word/the Christ, who first spoke creation into existence (Gen 1), dethrones the curse of sin and makes "all things new" again (Rev 21:5).

In summary then:

1. On Friday of creation week, God created mankind for the express purpose of reigning with God as rulers of God's creation, an assignment for which man disqualified himself

by sinning and thereby subjecting creation to the corrosive curse of sin.

2. On Friday of passion week, Pilate debated with the Jews over whether Jesus was the King of the Jews and how Pilate should treat that King, following which Pilate crucified Jesus, the reason for which Jesus came to earth, and by which ghastly death, Jesus broke the power of that curse of sin and began the process of making all things new.

3. In Ps 93, the Friday psalm, the author celebrates God, the King, the very subject of Pilate's debate and anticipates the drama of the crucifixion of Good Friday, five hundred years later, during which the King of the Jews submits to inundation by the waters of sin but demonstrates his superior power by prevailing over that smothering slime.

The parallels between Friday of creation week, Friday of passion week, and the Friday psalm are subtle, complex, but undeniable. God alone is the author of this drama.

9.

The Seventh Day (Saturday)

ON SATURDAY, THE SEVENTH day of creation week, Gen 2 tells us this:

> Thus the heavens and the earth were finished, and all the host of them. And on the seventh day God ended his work which he had made; and he rested on the seventh day from all his work which he had made. And God blessed the seventh day, and sanctified it: because that in it he had rested from all his work which God created and made. (vv. 1–3)

On Saturday of creation week, then, all God's creative work was done, the monumental tasks complete, and God rested. In the proverbial week of creation, stupendous, unparalleled work was finished—the results, amazing indeed.

Read in the context of what John and Paul later tell us, the Word of God, the preincarnate Christ, Jesus himself, was that aspect of God's person that had spoken the world, all of it, into existence. John says,

> In the beginning was the Word, and the Word was with God, and the Word was God. The same was in the beginning with God. *All things were made by him; and without him was not any thing made that was made.* (John 1:1–3, emphasis added)

Likewise, Paul says,

> Who hath delivered us from the power of darkness, and hath translated us into the kingdom of his dear Son: In whom we have redemption through his blood, even the forgiveness of sins: Who is the image of the invisible God, the firstborn of every creature: *For by him were all things created, that are in heaven, and that are in earth, visible and invisible, whether they be thrones, or dominions, or principalities, or powers: all things were created by him, and for him: And he is before all things, and by him all things consist.* (Col 1:13–17, emphasis added)

Consequently, John and Paul agree that, when Gen 1 and 2 describe creation, Genesis tells us of the work of Christ himself. The perfect, unmarred world existing before the fall of Gen 3 was "made" by the preincarnate Jesus, whom John calls the Word.

When all this is blended together, Genesis, the Gospel of John, and Paul's letter to the Colossians tell us Christ rested on the seventh day (Saturday) of creation week and the work he had completed was awe inspiring, or in a word, perfect.

The psalm of the day for Saturday is Ps 92. Psalm 92 is so connected to Saturday that in many, perhaps most, translations, it bears the title "A Psalm or Song for the Sabbath Day." The psalm was sung as accompaniment to the drink offering that occurred in the temple as the first lamb was offered in the Sabbath worship service.[1] This is how Ps 92 reads:

> *It is a good thing to give thanks unto the Lord, and to sing praises unto thy name, O Most High:*
> To shew forth thy lovingkindness in the morning, and thy faithfulness every night,
> Upon an instrument of ten strings, and upon the psaltery; upon the harp with a solemn sound.
> *For thou, Lord, hast made me glad through thy work: I will triumph in the works of thy hands.*

---

1. Phillips, *Exploring the Psalms*, 2:37.

O Lord, how great are thy works! and thy thoughts are very deep.

A brutish man knoweth not; neither doth a fool understand this.

When the wicked spring as the grass, and when all the workers of iniquity do flourish; it is that they shall be destroyed for ever:

But thou, LORD, art most high for evermore.

For, lo, thine enemies, O LORD, for, lo, thine enemies shall perish; all the workers of iniquity shall be scattered.

But my horn shalt thou exalt like the horn of an unicorn: I shall be anointed with fresh oil.

Mine eye also shall see my desire on mine enemies, and mine ears shall hear my desire of the wicked that rise up against me.

The righteous shall flourish like the palm tree: he shall grow like a cedar in Lebanon.

Those that be planted in the house of the LORD shall flourish in the courts of our God.

They shall still bring forth fruit in old age; they shall be fat and flourishing;

To shew that the LORD is upright: he is my rock, and there is no unrighteousness in him. (Emphasis added.)

Given the psalm's connection to the Sabbath, the Jewish holy day, and the reason for the Jew's celebration of the Sabbath (the completion of God's work of creation and his consequent rest), it is no stretch to conclude that the works of God (vv. 4–5), which are the *raison d'etre* for the praise of v. 1, are the works of God in creation week, works which are complete by day seven, Saturday.

Remember that Genesis's creation narrative is traditionally attributed to Moses, delivered by him shortly after the Jews' delivery from Egyptian slavery. The recently emancipated Jews have been told by Moses that their emancipator, their God, is the Creator, he who made their world. In other words they "know him." And on Sabbath of creation week, looking at what God accomplished in creation, especially before the fall brought the curse of sin, the view of God's great works had to prompt the thought that is considered the theme of Ps 92: "Praise the Savior, Ye who Know him."[2]

On Saturday of passion week, this is what Matthew records:

> Now the next day, that followed the day of the prepa-
> ration, the chief priests and Pharisees came together
> unto Pilate, Saying, Sir, we remember that that deceiver
> said, while he was yet alive, After three days I will rise
> again. Command therefore that the sepulchre be made
> sure until the third day, lest his disciples come by night,
> and steal him away, and say unto the people, He is risen
> from the dead: so the last error shall be worse than the
> first. Pilate said unto them, Ye have a watch: go your way,
> make it as sure as ye can. So they went, and made the
> sepulchre sure, sealing the stone, and setting a watch.
> (Matt 27:62–66)

Luke adds this:

> And the women also, which came with him from Gali-
> lee, followed after, and beheld the sepulchre, and how his
> body was laid. And they returned, and prepared spices
> and ointments; and rested the sabbath day according to
> the commandment. (Luke 23:55–56)

In a word, on Saturday of passion week, the Sabbath, Jesus rested in the tomb, just as on Saturday of creation week, the Sabbath, the Christ rested after completing creation.

The day before, as he died on the cruel cross, Jesus cried out with a loud voice and gave up the ghost (Matt 27:50; Mark 15:37). What was his loud cry? John says it was "*tetelestai*," a word which means, "It is finished" (John 19:30).[3] What did Jesus mean by that cryptic final word? What was finished? What had been accomplished?

The answer can perhaps be found not in the Gospels but in Revelation. There Christ upon his return "sat upon the throne [and] said, Behold, I make all things new" (Rev 21:5). In the epic

2. Phillips, *Exploring the Psalms*, 2:36.

3. Barclay, *Gospel of John*, 301.

film *The Passion of the Christ*, that phrase is transposed to the crucifixion. Jesus tells Mary, his mother, as he struggles to heft his cross to Calvary, that he, Jesus, is "making all things new."[4]

And, in David's great psalm describing the spiritual death of Jesus, Ps 69, the mystical subject of the song says, "I am forced to restore what I did not steal" (v. 4 NIV). That subtle phrasing describes the Creator Christ, whose perfect creation was fouled by man's sin, and who then died to restore that perfect world. Christ created it, but Christ did not steal its perfection. Man did. Man stole it; Christ did not. But Christ must restore it. In other words, Christ on the cross is "forced to restore what [he] did not steal." And that phrase says the equivalent of "I am making all things new." Jesus, the Word of God, spoke creation into existence (John 1, Gen 1), and creation was perfect. Man's sin spoiled creation, and Jesus, the Word of God, must make creation new, and perfect, again. Jesus is "forced to restore what [he] did not steal" (Ps 69:4).

Now "making all things new" is not yet complete, but the heavy lifting is done. ("TETELESTAI!") The sacrifice of Jesus wins the ultimate battle to restore perfection to creation, but the final work will be accomplished when Jesus returns, after we who live after him have enjoyed (or endured) a period during which we may commit to him or deny him.

In summary:

1. On Saturday, the Sabbath of creation week, Creator God, the Word of God, rested from his work of creation during that arduous creation process.

2. On Saturday, the Sabbath of passion week, Creator God, the Word of God, rested from the arduous work of passion week wherein he (Jesus) did the heavy lifting involved in "making all things new," redeeming creation, and restoring its perfection.

3. In the psalm of the day, Ps 92, selected centuries before Jesus, the psalmist praised the Savior for his work in creation.

4. Gibson, *Passion of the Christ*.

The common theme continues through Saturday. On Saturday in both creation week and passion week, the Creator rests after completing the arduous tasks of creating, while in the Saturday psalm of the day the psalmist praises the divine work of creation. One intelligence not bound by time, certainly not by men spread over the ages, inspired this seemingly disparate, and temporally remote, Scripture. And the correlation of creation week, passion week, and the psalms of the day prove this conclusively. It could happen no other way.

God made the selections; God is the author.

10.

The Eighth Day (Easter Sunday)

WE ARE BACK TO Sunday, the first day of the week, and passion week concludes with the greatest day in human history, Easter Sunday, the resurrection day of the Savior. Because it is Sunday, the first day of the week, the parallel Scripture for creation week is the same as Palm Sunday's, and the psalm of the day is, again, Ps 24.

On Sunday, the first day of creation week, Gen 1 tells us,

> In the beginning God created the heaven and the earth. And the earth was without form, and void; and darkness was upon the face of the deep. And the Spirit of God moved upon the face of the waters. And God said, Let there be light: and there was light. And God saw the light, that it was good: and God divided the light from the darkness. And God called the light Day, and the darkness he called Night. And the evening and the morning were the first day. (vv. 1–5)

Per Gen 1, then, on the first day of creation, Sunday, God created day and night, speaking them into existence, an event accomplished through the introduction of light. "Speaking" light into existence, amplified through John's Gospel, entails two revelations. First, Jesus is the Word—in Gen 1 the spoken word—and by him "all things were made . . . and without him was not anything made that was made" (John 1:3). Second, as Jesus speaks "light" into existence, John tells us that Jesus is, in fact, the "light of the world."

> In him was life; and the life was the light of men. And the light shineth in darkness; and the darkness comprehended it not. There was a man sent from God, whose name was John. The same came for a witness, to bear witness of the Light, that all men through him might believe. He was not that Light, but was sent to bear witness of that Light. That was the true Light, which lighteth every man that cometh into the world. (John 1:4–9)

These then are the events of the first day of creation, as amplified by the Gospel of John. Jesus, the Christ, the Word of God and the Light, entered into the void that existed before creation. And then he created!

The Light of the World entered. And beginning with that, everything changed. That is the focus of day one of creation.

The psalm of the day for Sunday, selected by the Jewish priests in approximately 500 BC, was Ps 24.

Psalm 24 is a psalm of David, written by the shepherd king to celebrate a very special event in the history of the Jewish state, the glorious day on which David brought into his new capital, Jerusalem, the ark of the covenant. The ark, as discussed throughout this work, represents both God's presence among his people and his home. This is important: the ark represents, even is, the presence of God himself. It was constructed, in fact, in God's own words, "so that I may live among" my people (Exod 25:8).

Psalm 24, then, celebrates the entry of God himself into Jerusalem.

David was so exhilarated at bringing God's lodging, his very presence, within the Jerusalem walls that he penned Ps 24 to memorialize the portentous event. This, in part, is what David wrote:

> Lift up your heads, O ye gates; and be ye lifted up, ye everlasting doors; and the King of glory shall come in.
> Who is this King of glory? The LORD strong and mighty, the LORD mighty in battle.

71

> Lift up your heads, O ye gates; even lift them up, ye
> everlasting doors; and the King of glory shall come in.
> Who is this King of glory? The LORD of hosts, he is
> the King of glory. Selah. (Ps 24:7–10)

In the psalm of the day for Sunday, then, David celebrates bringing the ark into Jerusalem. The ark represents God's dwelling, his very presence, and David has brought him into David's capital city. It is momentous! Indeed, David announces grandly that through the gates of Jerusalem, through its everlasting doors, David has brought the "King of glory[,] . . . the LORD strong and mighty, . . . the LORD of hosts."

On the first Sunday of passion week, Palm Sunday, we saw that Jesus, the Christ, the Word, the Son of God, entered Jerusalem. The connection to Ps 24 was transparently clear. Now that same connection to resurrection day, Easter Sunday, is evident. Jesus has left the empty tomb, left the somnolence of the dead, and reentered Jerusalem. Psalm 24's context and content fit Easter Sunday as surely as Palm Sunday. The mind that, five hundred years earlier, selected Ps 24 as the Sunday psalm knew that Ps 24, David's ebullient, triumphant pronouncement that "the King of Glory," "the LORD strong and mighty," had entered Jerusalem's gates would fit the momentous events of both Palm Sunday and Easter Sunday. No human mind could have anticipated the events of passion week, 500 years later.

Only God could have done it.

11.

Conclusion

THE RESULTS OF THIS exercise should be conclusive, should be *proof*. Seven out of seven days in creation week, and more importantly passion week, directly coincide with the background and content of the psalms of the day. Indeed, the count is actually eight for eight; for the Sunday psalm, Ps 24, fits both Easter Sunday and Palm Sunday.

Indeed, one previously unmentioned peculiarity, one that actually supports the divine premise, is the fact that for many of the seven days, the connection of the psalm to the events of passion week, five hundred years in the future, are more obvious than the correlation to creation week (eons in the past), the admitted pattern used by the priests to craft *Shir shel yom*. The priests knew they patterned their choices after creation week; they could not know, however, that their choices would more closely fit passion week. The Sunday psalm is perhaps the prime example: Psalm 24 fits passion week's Sundays much better than it fits the first day of Gen 1's creation.

To even the casual mind, the likelihood of temple priests in 500 BC selecting at random seven psalms that would correspond to daily events to transpire five hundred years later seems impossible. But, when the problem is approached systematically and mathematically, the likelihood belies any chance of accidental occurrence. The problem becomes a mathematical exercise in computing permutations and/or combinations.

The first step in such a calculation is to determine how many combinations of seven psalms could be formed from the set of psalms from which the seven are to be drawn. That helps to establish the odds of any combination of psalms being chosen as the specific seven to be assigned the seven days of the week. One must calculate the number of different combinations of seven psalms that were possible when the priests sat down in 500 BC to select the exact seven they would use. The mathematical formula for that calculation is

> n to the r power, where n = the number of things to choose from and r = the number to be chosen

In this instance, there are one hundred and fifty psalms, so "n," the number of things to choose from, is one hundred and fifty. One hundred fifty is our "n." And the number of psalms to be chosen is seven, that is, seven psalms to be selected from the one hundred and fifty total psalms. Our equation (n to the r power) then is this:

> 150 X 150 X 150 X 150 X 150 X 150 X 150 = the number of different combinations that could be compiled from the 150 psalms in the psaltery

The product of that intimidating calculation is

> 1,708,593,750,000,000

That breathtaking number represents the number of different combinations of seven psalms that can be created from a set of psalms numbering one hundred and fifty. This means that the likelihood of the psalms of the day being selected in that sequence by mere happenstance is one chance in 1,708,593,750,000,000.

That stunning statement bears repeating: the likelihood of the psalms of the day selected by chance being the very seven, in the exact order, which the temple priests gave us in 500 BC is one chance in 1,708,593,750,000,000. And that computation takes into account only the mathematical likelihood that the specific combination of Pss 24, 48, 82, 94, 81, 93, and 92 would be selected at random by those priests.

Those odds are prohibitive. In other words, it could not have happened by chance.[1]

But the mathematical odds, as prohibitive as they are, are not the end of this astonishing inquiry. This computation tells us how unlikely would be a serendipitous selection of these seven psalms as the psalms of the day, but it speaks not at all to the fact that the events of passion week, day by day, correspond mystically with the themes of the palms of the day. The calculation does not take into consideration the fact that the circumstances behind the seven psalms of the day would correspond to the actual narrative events of those days in passion week, five centuries in the future. That synchronicity is more astonishing than the prohibitive odds of random selection.

This is true even given the uncertainty of the size of the then-Psaltery from which the priests made their selections. While the selection odds might be marginally improved by a smaller psaltery, the mere combination odds do not explain the fact that the seven psalms of the day hauntingly anticipate with predictive accuracy the events of passion week, a week that will not occur until five hundred years later. That fact cannot be explained by even the remotest of odds. That predictive accuracy means that God Almighty, with knowledge of the future, and not the mortal Jewish priests,

---

1. In candor I must, however, offer a parenthetical: The figure here is one chance in 1,708,593,750,000,000. That appears to be the likelihood of seven psalms from a one hundred and fifty psalm musical psaltery being selected in the precise combination of 24, 48, 82, 94, 81, 93, and 92. Even so, that is but an approximation, based upon the assumption that when the priests made their selection, the Psaltery had already reached its present, completed size of one hundred and fifty psalms. If on that date of selection five hundred years before Christ the number was smaller than one hundred and fifty, then the odds are somewhat different—better, one might say—but they are still prohibitive. In that case, the odds of the precise combination are perhaps improved, but those odds remain impossibly prohibitive. The combination of seven psalms of the day, whether selected from a psaltery of one hundred and fifty or one hundred, could not be chosen by mere chance.

selected these psalms. And when God selected the psalms of the week, God patterned them after the most historically important week in all history, passion week, during which Jesus, "the Word" of John 1, created yet again, "made all things new" (Rev 21:5).

Why should the mental exercise of this little book matter? Does it matter? What does it mean? Is it merely interesting lagniappe to capture our imaginations and titillate our wonder?

I think not.

Instead, I believe recognition of this startling phenomenon is desperately needed in our modern epoch, a time that social wags call a "post-Christian era," as if in this day of intellectual skepticism Christian faith is obsolete. If faith cannot be proven, say the skeptical, it is to be discarded in an age in which proof, not baseless belief, carries the day.

Well, here *is* proof, God's proof. *Shir shel yom*, the psalm of the day, is proof. If God did not select the psalms of the day and script the events of passion week, then who did? This haunting consanguinity between the weeks in Scripture and the psalms of the day is proof, undeniable proof. Even the skeptics of our supposedly post-Christian era must, I suggest, accept it or explain it.

We *should* of course believe on faith. As Jesus told the doubting Thomas, "Blessed are those who have not seen [proof] and yet have believed" (John 20:29). Even so, we have skeptics to this day, doubting Thomases, if you will, and they, like Thomas, must, we hope, believe after seeing God's proof. For God has given us that proof! And that proof, part of it at least, is found in the weeks in Scripture.

Simply put, God wrote the book: *he gave us proof!*

And with such proof, the only logical response is belief.

Bibliography

Alcorn, Randy. Heaven. Carol Stream, IL: Tyndale, 2004.

Apple, Raymond. "The Psalms of the Day." Jewish Bible Quarterly 42.2 (Apr.–June 2014) 114–20.

Barclay, William. The Gospel of John. 2nd ed. The Daily Bible Study Series 2. Philadelphia: Westminster, 1956.

Gibson, Mel, dir. The Passion of the Christ. Los Angeles: 20th Century Studios, 2004. DVD.

Phillips, John. Exploring the Psalms. 2 vols. New York: Loizeaux Brothers, 1988.

www.ingramcontent.com/pod-product-compliance
Lightning Source LLC
LaVergne TN
LVHW021618080426
835510LV00019B/2631